MW01598978

"Need-to-read inside in ... ne -
the best source in the b ... ,

"The Inside the Minds ... , and
techniques of accomplished professionals..." – Chuck Birenbaum, Partner, Thelen
Reid & Priest

"Aspatore has tapped into a gold mine of knowledge and expertise ignored by
other publishing houses." – Jack Barsky, Managing Director, Information
Technology & Chief Information Officer, ConEdison *Solutions*

"Unlike any other publisher – actual authors that are on the front-lines of what is
happening in industry." – Paul A. Sellers, Executive Director, National Sales, Fleet
and Remarketing, Hyundai Motor America

"A snapshot of everything you need..." – Charles Koob, Co-Head of Litigation
Department, Simpson Thacher & Bartlet

"Everything good books should be - honest, informative, inspiring, and incredibly
well-written." – Patti D. Hill, President, BlabberMouth PR

"Great information for both novices and experts." – Patrick Ennis, Partner,
ARCH Venture Partners

"A rare peek behind the curtains and into the minds of the industry's best." –
Brandon Baum, Partner, Cooley Godward

"Intensely personal, practical advice from seasoned dealmakers." – Mary Ann
Jorgenson, Coordinator of Business Practice Area, Squire, Sanders & Dempsey

"Great practical advice and thoughtful insights." – Mark Gruhin, Partner,
Schmeltzer, Aptaker & Shepard, PC

"Reading about real-world strategies from real working people beats the typical
business book hands down." - Andrew Ceccon, Chief Marketing Officer,
OnlineBenefits Inc.

"Books of this publisher are syntheses of actual experiences of real-life, hands-on,
front-line leaders--no academic or theoretical nonsense here. Comprehensive,
tightly organized, yet nonetheless motivational!" - Lac V. Tran, Sr. Vice President,
CIO and Associate Dean Rush University Medical Center

"Aspatore is unlike other publishers...books feature cutting-edge information
provided by top executives working on the front-line of an industry." - Debra
Reisenthel, President and CEO, Novasys Medical Inc

ASPATORE

www.Aspatore.com

Aspatore Books, a Thomson Reuters business, is the largest and most exclusive publisher of C-level executives (CEO, CFO, CTO, CMO, partner) from the world's most respected companies and law firms. Aspatore annually publishes a select group of C-level executives from the Global 1,000, top 250 law firms (partners and chairs), and other leading companies of all sizes. C-Level Business Intelligence™, as conceptualized and developed by Aspatore Books, provides professionals of all levels with proven business intelligence from industry insiders—direct and unfiltered insight from those who know it best— as opposed to third-party accounts offered by unknown authors and analysts. Aspatore Books is committed to publishing an innovative line of business and legal books, those which lay forth principles and offer insights that, when employed, can have a direct financial impact on the reader's business objectives, whatever they may be. In essence, Aspatore publishes critical tools—need-to-read as opposed to nice-to-read books—for all business professionals.

Inside the Minds

The critically acclaimed *Inside the Minds* series provides readers of all levels with proven business intelligence from C-level executives (CEO, CFO, CTO, CMO, partner) from the world's most respected companies. Each chapter is comparable to a white paper or essay and is a future-oriented look at where an industry/profession/topic is heading and the most important issues for future success. Each author has been selected based upon their experience and C-level standing within the professional community. *Inside the Minds* was conceived in order to give readers actual insights into the leading minds of business executives worldwide. Because so few books or other publications are actually written by executives in industry, *Inside the Minds* presents an unprecedented look at various industries and professions never before available.

I N S I D E   T H E   M I N D S

DUI Law Enforcement Strategies

Law Enforcement Officials on Administering Field Sobriety Tests, Interpreting Results, and Preparing for Court Testimony

ASPATORE

Mat #40772646

BOOK & ARTICLE IDEA SUBMISSIONS

If you are a C-Level executive, senior lawyer, or venture capitalist interested in submitting a book or article idea to the Aspatore editorial board for review, please e-mail TLR.AspatoreAuthors@thomson.com. Aspatore is especially looking for highly specific ideas that would have a direct financial impact on behalf of a reader. Completed publications can range from 2 to 2,000 pages. Include your book/article idea, biography, and any additional pertinent information.

ISBN 978-0-314-19910-2

For corrections, updates, comments or any other inquiries please e-mail
TLR.AspatoreEditorial@thomson.com.

First Printing, 2008
10 9 8 7 6 5 4 3 2 1

CONTENTS

The Essentials of DUI Assessment and Testing

Darrell E. Fisher

Lieutenant Colonel and Assistant Superintendant

Nebraska State Patrol

ASPATORE

Training

Detection of alcohol- and drug-impaired driving and apprehension of the driver are complex and demanding law enforcement responsibilities, sufficient to warrant a separate curriculum. To meet the basic challenges for law enforcement to combat DUI (driving under the influence) violations, the National Highway Traffic Safety Administration has developed the following three modules that address impaired driving (both alcohol- and basic drug-impaired driving):

- *DWI Detection and Standardized Field Sobriety Testing,* with a core curriculum consisting of sixteen sessions that span twenty-two hours and forty-five minutes of instruction, excluding breaks. With breaks and meal periods, the course requires three full training days. The participants will recognize driving behaviors and other indicators commonly exhibited by impaired drivers (Phase One); know and recognize typical clues of alcohol and drug impairment that may be detected during face-to-face contact with DUI suspects (Phase Two); know and perform the appropriate administrative procedures and recognize typical clues of alcohol impairment that may be seen during administration of the three standardized field sobriety tests (Horizontal Gaze Nystagmus, Walk-and-Turn, and One Leg Stand); and understand the DUI prosecution requirements and their relevance to DWI (driving while intoxicated)/DUI arrest reporting.
- *Introduction to Drugs That Impair,* a four-hour overview of drugs other than alcohol that impair.
- *Drugs That Impair Driving,* an eight-hour module that provides officers with information on the general observable signs of drug-impaired drivers. This module was developed to increase officer awareness of signs of drug impairment and the need to make referrals to drug recognition experts (DREs).

In 1986, the Advisory Committee on Highway Safety of the International Association of Chiefs of Police (IACP) passed a resolution that recommended law enforcement agencies adopt and implement the field sobriety testing training program developed by the National Highway Traffic Safety Administration (NHTSA). As the program has grown, it has become apparent that to ensure continued success, nationally accepted standards must be established. These standards, which establish criteria for the selection and training of SFST (standardized field sobriety test) practitioners, would help ensure the continued high level of success of the SFST program.

In 1992, the IACP Highway Safety Committee recommended the development of this system of nationally accepted standards. A committee was formed, including senior SFST instructors from several states, curriculum specialists, and training administrators. This committee met in working groups and reached a consensus concerning the many issues relating to the SFST program, and developed recommended minimum standards presented to the IACP Advisory Committee on Highway Safety. The standards were presented and approved by the Highway Safety Committee in June 1992.

Training for law enforcement officers on DUI procedures is relative to the agency. Some law enforcement agencies have concluded that entry-level positions receive training relative to the statutory requirements and fundamental detection, arrest, and processing. Those agencies concluded the specific subject-matter training (i.e., SFSTs) should be offered only to officers who have amassed substantial on-the-job experience in detecting and arresting impaired drivers. Other agencies have advanced equally strong arguments to support the position that the training is appropriate for recruit-level officers. Either assessment is left to the individual agencies training in the standardized curriculum.

However, all user agencies should note that the ability to maintain the skills learned in the standardized curriculum will rapidly diminish if they are not reinforced by frequent "street" application and occasional in-service training. This is not to imply this training is so complex or confusing that only exceptionally skilled officers can master it. The techniques of DUI detection and use of the SFSTs can readily be grasped by anyone of average competence, provided they are willing to devote the appropriate time and effort to study and practice. The SFSTs are skills, not unlike defensive tactics, firearms training, or pursuit driving skills; they require practice and training to develop proficiency.

The fundamental purpose of the training is to foster DUI deterrence—i.e., to dissuade people from driving while impaired—by increasing the odds they will be arrested and convicted. The course is based on the assumption that a principal reason for enforcing DUI laws is to deter those who might otherwise be tempted to break the law. If potential DUI violators believe there is a real risk of being caught, it is reasonable to believe most will refrain from driving while impaired.

Police officers cannot possibly detect and arrest all DUI violators. Not all who are arrested will be convicted and punished. However, officers can improve the skills that increase the chances of detecting, arresting, recording, articulating, and gathering sufficient evidence to sustain a conviction.

The above training is based on the premise that officers perform two fundamental tasks that affect the likelihood of apprehending and convicting impaired drivers. The first of those tasks is *detection*. Detection is defined as "the entire process of identifying and gathering evidence to determine whether a suspect should be arrested for DUI." DUI detection begins when an officer's attention is drawn to a particular vehicle or its operator. The precipitating events are unlimited. The initial "spark" that causes the officer to focus attention on the particular vehicle may carry with it an immediate, strong suspicion of the possibility of impairment, only a slight suspicion of the possibility of impairment, or, depending on the circumstances, no suspicion at all at the time. Regardless, it sets in motion a process in which the officer focuses on the particular individual and has the opportunity to observe and elicit additional evidence.

The detection process ends only when the officer formulates the decision either to arrest or not to arrest the individual for DUI. That decision is based on all the accumulated evidence. Effective DUI enforcers do not leap immediately to the arrest/no arrest decision. Rather, they proceed carefully through a series of intermediate decisions, each of which can elicit evidence. The *DWI Detection and Standardized Field Sobriety Testing* course clearly outlines each decision step.

Successful DUI detectors are those officers who know what to look and listen for and who have the skills to ask the right questions and to choose and use the right tests. They are highly motivated and apply their knowledge and skill whenever they contact someone who may be under the influence. In this way, they tend to make more DUI arrests and gather the best possible evidence to support their charges.

The second basic task of effective DUI enforcement is *description*. Just as detection is the process of collecting evidence, description is the process of articulating evidence. Successful description demands the ability to verbally convey evidence clearly and convincingly. The officer's challenge is to communicate observational evidence to people who were not there to see, hear, or smell the evidence themselves. The officer's tools are words. These words make up the written report and verbal testimony the officer uses to "paint a word picture" when communicating with the prosecutor, the judge, the members of the jury, and the defense attorney. This skill allows these people to develop a sharp mental image that allows them to "see," "hear," and "smell" the evidence. Successful DUI describers have the verbal skills needed to use descriptive words and phrases to communicate their evidence clearly and convincingly.

The *DWI Detection and Standardized Field Sobriety Testing* course trains officers to become more skillful at detection and description, make more DUI arrests, and obtain more convictions. These actions will lead to greater DUI deterrence through less impaired driving and fewer motor vehicle crashes, injuries, and deaths.

In support of SFST training, the NHTSA has developed a self-instructional SFST refresher training course, using an interactive CD-ROM as the delivery technology. SFST refresher training can now take place anywhere, anytime, using a desktop personal computer, or a laptop computer when offsite. This training targets law enforcement officers at the federal, state, county, and local levels who have already taken and successfully completed the basic SFST classroom training course. These individuals are now able to refresh their skills at:

- Recognizing and interpreting evidence of DUI
- Administering and interpreting the scientifically validated sobriety tests
- Describing DUI evidence clearly and convincingly

The refresher training course provides the user with information regarding recent case law and research studies conducted. Also, it outlines the availability of advanced training in recognizing and understanding the characteristics of drugs that impair driving. There is even a separate section of the refresher training course designated specifically for prosecutors. It is intended to assist them in understanding the concepts and principles of SFST.

The above refresher course notwithstanding, each agency should designate updated refresher training for SFSTs at least every other year. This biennial cycle allows the officers to demonstrate proficiency in this skilled area. Without repetition and the subsequent demonstration of proficiency on a biennial basis, skills may diminish and/or bad habits set in, and quality control and integrity in the program are lost.

Ensuring High-Quality Written Documentation

Successful prosecution depends on the clarity and completeness with which the arresting officer's observations are presented. The arresting officer must be able to convey observations with sufficient clarity to convince others there was probable cause to believe the suspect was under the influence of alcohol and/or drugs. The officer's efforts in detecting, apprehending, investigating, arresting, and testing DUI offenders are of little value if the officer cannot document sufficient evidence to prove each element of the DUI offense. Corroborative chemical test evidence, as well as additional evidence gathered subsequent to the arrest, may be suppressed if the arresting officer does not adequately establish probable cause for the arrest prior to the chemical test. A clear, concise report will enable the officer to recall those details and present them through direct testimony.

Evidence must be clearly conveyed in the subsequent written narrative offense/arrest report. A well-written, clear, and convincing narrative report increases the likelihood that a conviction will result because:

- The prosecutor is more likely to file the charge if the evidence is organized, clearly documented, and compelling.
- The defense is less likely to contest the charge when the report is descriptive, detailed, and complete.

- A well-written, clear, and convincing narrative report helps ensure recall later if the matter goes to trial and facilitates better testimony in court.

The written report should document all evidence available to establish the essential ingredients of the prosecution's case. It should clearly articulate that probable cause existed for the arrest:

1. The accused was the operator or in actual physical control of the vehicle.
2. There was reasonable suspicion for stopping/contacting the accused.
3. There was probable cause to believe the accused was impaired.

Furthermore, the written report should document that proper arrest procedures for a DUI case were followed, and the rights of the accused were protected according to the laws of the jurisdiction where the arrest occurred. The report should highlight the subsequent observations and interview of the accused, as well as the request and subsequent results of the corroborative evidence (chemical testing).

The narrative report should be organized around the total sequence of events, beginning at the first observation of the offender, continuing through the arrest, and culminating with the incarceration or the release of the subject. Any DUI investigation field notes describing the evidence observed during the three phases of detection greatly assist preparation of the narrative offense/arrest report. Observation and results recorded on the field notes can refresh the officer's memory when preparing the narrative report.

Report writing is an essential skill for every police officer, but good report writing becomes second nature with practice. While there is no one best way to write a report, it is helpful to follow a uniform format. Officers should be guided by departmental policies and/or instructions or requirements specified by the prosecutor in their geographic areas of responsibility. Below is a suggested report format for officers to follow.

Suggested Report Writing Format

1. Establish venue: the officer's name, department, the jurisdiction the officer was working, and where the stop took place.

2. Initial observations
   - First observations of the offender and their actions
   - Factors that drew officer's attention
   - Time and location of first observations

3. Vehicle stop
   - Unusual actions taken
   - Offender's response to the stop command
   - Method(s) officer used to signal the stop command
   - The fashion in which the offender stopped the vehicle

4. Face-to-face contact
   - The suspect's personal appearance
   - The condition of the suspect's eyes, speech, etc.
   - The names, numbers, seating locations of any passengers
   - Any unusual actions taken
   - Any unusual statements made
   - What the officer saw, heard, and smelled

5. Operation/actual physical control
   - Establish the suspect as the individual seated in the driver's seat, behind the steering wheel, and in possession of the keys to the vehicle, or proof that keys are not required to start the vehicle.

6. Exit from the vehicle
   - Does the suspect forget to unfasten the seat belt?
   - Was the suspect unable to open the door?
   - Does the suspect leave the vehicle in gear?
   - Does the suspect put hands on door, roof, steering wheel, or seat back to lift them out of the car?
   - Does the suspect fall back against the side of the car upon exiting?
   - Does the suspect stop to straighten his or her clothes?
   - Does the suspect keep a hand on the car for steadiness while walking back to the patrol car?
   - Does the suspect stumble, fall, or nearly fall in the distance between the suspect's car and the patrol car?

7. Field sobriety tests
   - Physical performance
   - Mental performance
   - If a preliminary breath test was administered, the results should be noted here also.
8. The arrest
   - The time the suspect was notified of being under arrest
   - If any Implied Consent forms are read at roadside in conjunction with the arrest, it should be noted here.
9. Disposition of the suspect's vehicle
10. Disposition of passengers/property
11. Transport of offender
    - Departure time
    - Arrival time at the jail or detention or testing facility
12. Evidentiary tests
    - What test(s) were requested and administered
    - Who administered the test(s)
    - Test results, if available
13. Implied Consent/Miranda Admonitions
    - When given, and any witnesses should be noted
14. Statements of witnesses
15. Notification of suspect's attorney or other party, if required by jurisdictional rules
    - Time of call(s)
    - Result of call(s), if known
16. Citation(s)
    - Charges
    - Disposition of defendant's copy
17. Incarceration or release
    - Time
    - If released, to whom
18. Transfer of chemical test to laboratory, if required
    - If placed in evidence, the time, date, and technician or lab scientist who took possession
    - If packaged and mailed, the certified mail receipt and when executed.

Signs and Observations

The observations made by the officer during a typical traffic contact that could culminate in a DUI arrest develop in three phases:

1. Vehicle in motion
2. Personal contact
3. Pre-arrest screening

Each phase of the typical traffic contact may develop valuable information or evidence for the officer.

Phase One: Vehicle in Motion

Vehicle in motion consists of the initial observations of vehicular operation, the stop decision that may be made, and the observation of the stop. The initial observation of vehicle operation begins when the officer first notices the vehicle and/or the driver. If the initial observation discloses vehicle maneuvers or human behaviors that may be associated with alcohol and/or drug influence, the officer may develop an initial suspicion the driver may be DUI. Typical examples include:

• Moving traffic violation (running stop sign or traffic signal, improper/unsafe passing due to oncoming traffic, improper turn in front of oncoming or opposing traffic, following too closely, improper or unsafe lane changes or unsafe merging, weaving through traffic, crossing a double yellow traffic line, improper passing on the shoulder, excessive speed for conditions, etc.)
• Vehicle equipment violations (no tail lights or broken tail light reflector, no headlamps or broken headlamps, muffler violations, etc.)
• Expired vehicle registration renewal sticker
• Other driving actions (drifting within own lane, slower than normal speed, etc.)
• Drinking in the vehicle

Based on the officer's observation of the vehicle operation, the officer must decide whether reasonable suspicion exists to stop the vehicle. If the officer does not believe he or she has reasonable suspicion based on initial observations, the stop/no stop decision may be delayed to continue observing the vehicle. Whenever there is a valid reason to stop a vehicle, the officer should be alert to the possibility the driver may be impaired by alcohol and/or other drugs. If the officer does believe there is reasonable suspicion based on initial observations, the officer should execute the stop command and make a safe traffic stop.

Once the stop command has been communicated to the suspect driver, the officer must closely observe the driver's actions and vehicle maneuvers during the stopping sequence. Significant evidence of alcohol/drug influence comes to light during the stopping sequence, as the officer turning on the patrol vehicle's emergency lights creates a simple test of the suspect's driving impairment. In some cases, the stopping sequence itself may produce the first suspicion of DUI. Drivers impaired by alcohol and/or other drugs may respond in unexpected and dangerous ways to the stop command. The signal to stop requires the driver to process the signal to stop, respond to the signal by slowing, activate the turn signal, turn the steering wheel, operate the brake pedal, and negotiate a safe stop. However, once the officer gives the stop command, the impaired driver's tasks become more complex. If the suspect is under the influence of an intoxicant, the suspect may not be able to handle this more complex driving.

- Excessively slow/no response to the stop command
- Immediate stop in the traffic lane
- Rapid acceleration in attempt to avoid stop
- Striking or running over fixed objects at roadside

Phase Two: Personal Contact

Personal contact with the driver consists of the face-to-face observation and the interview of the driver while still in the vehicle, the officer's decision to instruct the driver to exit the vehicle, and the officer's observation of the driver's exit from the vehicle.

The interview/observation of the driver begins as soon as the suspect vehicle and the patrol car have come to complete stops, and continues through the officer's approach to the suspect vehicle. Prior to any face-to-face observation and the interview of the driver, the officer may have already developed a suspicion that the driver is impaired, based on the observations of the vehicle operation and of the stop. Alternately, the vehicle operation and the stop may have been fairly normal, and the officer may have no particular suspicion of DUI before the face-to-face contact; e.g., vehicle equipment violations or vehicle registration renewal sticker as outlined above during Phase One.

Regardless of what evidence may have come to light during Phase One, the initial face-to-face contact between the officer and the suspect usually provides the first definite indications that alcohol and/or drug impairment may be present. This phase requires the officer to use three senses to gather evidence of alcohol and/or other drug influence.

- Sense of sight
- Sense of hearing
- Sense of smell

Sight

There are a number of things the officer may see during the interview that are indicators of impairment by alcohol and/or drugs. Among them are:

- Bloodshot eyes
- Soiled clothing
- Fumbling/trembling fingers
- Alcoholic beverage containers in plain view
- Drugs or drug paraphernalia in plain view
- Bruises, bumps, or scratches
- Other unusual actions

Hearing

Things the officer may hear during the interview that are indicators of impairment by alcohol and/or drugs are:

- Slurred speech
- Admission of drinking or using drugs
- Inconsistent responses
- Impatient, abrupt, or abusive language
- Other unusual statements

Smell

Indicators the officer may smell during the interview that point to impairment by alcohol and/or drugs are:

- Odor of alcoholic beverages
- Odor of burnt marijuana
- Odor of incense, cologne, toothpaste, breath sprays, or other "cover-up" odors
- Other unusual odors

From this point on, officer safety is a paramount consideration for the officer. Observations begin for the officer immediately when the suspect's vehicle comes to a stop and continue through the officer's decision to instruct the suspect to exit the vehicle:

- Is the suspect reaching for something inside the vehicle, hiding contraband, displaying unusual/suspicious movements?
- Are there alcoholic beverage containers or drug paraphernalia in plain view?
- Does the suspect voluntarily lower his or her window, or does the officer have to rap on the window or signal the driver to open the window? Does the suspect lower rear window first, then open the front window part way? Does the suspect open the driver's door?
- Is there an odor of alcohol, cannabis, chemical, or other odors emanating from the open window/door?
- Does the suspect appear dazed or stuporous?
- Is the speech thick or slurred?
- Is the suspect impatient—"Is this going to take long?"

The questions an officer asks of the suspect and the way in which they are asked can provide simple, divided-attention tasks, based on the observations made above. For example, the officer will ask the suspect to produce his or her operator's license and vehicle registration. The officer should carefully observe the suspect's search patterns when responding to the request for the operator's license, vehicle registration, and proof of insurance.

- Does the suspect pass over the license?
- Does the suspect fumble or drop the wallet, license, or registration?
- Does the suspect hand the officer a credit card or inappropriate documents?
- Is the suspect unable to locate the vehicle registration and/or the proof of insurance?
- Does the suspect forget to produce the documents requested when the officer asks an interrupting or distracting question (unable to divide his or her attention)?
  - Would you please turn the ignition off?
  - Would you please turn your radio down?
  - Where are you traveling tonight?
- Does the suspect ignore the question because he or she is concentrating on the license/registration search (unable to divide his or her attention)?
- Does the suspect provide an incorrect answer to the question?

Ultimately, the officer's decision to instruct the suspect to exit the vehicle may be based on the results of those observations made from the questions above.

How the suspect exits the vehicle and the actions and behavior of the suspect during the exit sequence may provide important additional evidence of alcohol and/or other drug influence.

- Does the suspect forget to unfasten the seat belt?
- Does the suspect have difficulty opening the door?
- Does the suspect leave the vehicle in gear?

- Does the suspect put hands on door, roof, steering wheel, or seat back to lift himself or herself out of the car?
- Does the suspect fall back against the side of the car upon exiting?
- Does the suspect stop to straighten his or her clothes?
- Does the suspect keep a hand on the car for steadiness while walking back to the patrol car?
- Does the suspect stumble, fall, or nearly fall in the distance between the suspect's vehicle and the patrol car?

Phase Three: Pre-arrest Screening and Tests

Pre-arrest screening consists of structured, formal psychophysical testing and possibly a preliminary breath test, if available, of persons suspected of DUI, and culminates in the arrest/no arrest decision. Psychophysical tests are methods of assessing a suspect's mental and/or physical impairment. The most significant psychophysical tests are the standardized field sobriety tests, administered at roadside. The preliminary breath test can also be very important in helping corroborate all other evidence, in helping confirm the officer's judgment as to whether the suspect is under the influence, and in assisting the officer in determining whether alcohol is the intoxicant causing the impairment. Drugs other than alcohol will not produce a positive reading on a preliminary breath-testing instrument. Therefore, if the suspect performs poorly and is determined by the officer to be impaired, alcohol may be ruled out as the drug causing the suspect's impairment.

The SFSTs are used to determine intoxication or impairment, rather than to measure a specific blood-alcohol concentration (BAC). The purposes of administering these tests are to assist the officer in making a decision regarding arrest, to help establish probable cause for the arrest, and to constitute one element of evidence in the DUI proceeding.

For many years, law enforcement officers have utilized field sobriety tests to determine the impairment of a person's driving due to alcohol influence. The performance of the person on those field sobriety tests was used by the officer to develop probable cause for arrest, and as evidence in any subsequent court proceeding for DUI. A wide variety of field sobriety tests existed, and there was a need to develop a battery of standardized valid tests.

Beginning in late 1975, extensive scientific research studies were sponsored by the National Highway Traffic Safety Administration (NHTSA) through a contract with the Southern California Research Institute (SCRI) to determine which roadside field sobriety tests were the most accurate. SCRI traveled to law enforcement agencies throughout the United States to select the most commonly used field sobriety tests. Six tests were used in the initial stages of this study. Laboratory research indicated that three of these tests, when administered in a standardized manner, were a highly reliable battery of tests for distinguishing BACs above 0.10:

- Horizontal Gaze Nystagmus (HGN)
- Walk-and-Turn (WAT)
- One-Leg Stand (OLS)

NHTSA analyzed the laboratory test data and found:

- HGN, by itself, was 77 percent accurate.
- WAT, by itself, was 68 percent accurate.
- OLS, by itself, was 65 percent accurate.
- By combining the results of HGN and WAT, an 80 percent accuracy rate can be achieved.

The final phase of this study was conducted as a field validation. Standardized, practical, and effective procedures were developed. The tests were determined to discriminate in the field, as well as in the laboratory. The three standardized tests were found to be highly reliable in identifying subjects with BACs above 0.10. The results of the study validated the SFSTs. Since the original validation studies in the mid- to late 1970s, three SFST validation studies were undertaken between 1995 and 1998:

- Colorado in 1995
- Florida in 1997
- San Diego in 1998

The Florida and San Diego studies determined the SFSTs are valid and reliable indices of the presence of alcohol at 0.08 BAC limits. These studies also determined the SFST three-test battery is the only scientifically validated and reliable method for discriminating between impaired and unimpaired drivers.

Procedures for Administering the Roadside Tests

Horizontal Gaze Nystagmus

Nystagmus is defined as an involuntary jerking of the eyes. Specifically, Horizontal Gaze Nystagmus is an involuntary jerking of the eyes occurring as the eyes gaze to the side. In addition to being involuntary, the person is generally unaware that it is happening and powerless to stop it. It cannot be practiced or controlled; hence, HGN is the most reliable indicator of a neurological dysfunction, one cause of which is the ingestion of alcohol or certain other drugs.

It is important to administer the HGN test systematically, using the following steps to ensure that the test is performed properly and consistently.

Step I: Check for Eyeglasses

Begin by instructing the suspect to remove his or her eyeglasses, if worn. It does not matter whether the suspect can see the stimulus with perfect clarity, as long as the suspect can see it at all. It is not a vision test.

Step II: Verbal Instructions

Tell the suspect you are going to check his or her eyes. Ask the suspect to:

- Stand, with feet together, hands at the sides
- Keep head still
- Look at the stimulus
- Follow the movement of the stimulus with eyes only (not turning head)
- Keep looking at the stimulus until told the test is over

Step III: Positioning the Stimulus

For officer safety purposes, the stimulus used should be in the officer's non-weapon hand. Position the stimulus approximately twelve to fifteen inches in front of the suspect's nose and slightly above eye level to commence the test.

Step IV: Check for Equal Pupil Size and Resting Nystagmus

The pupils of the eyes should be equal in size, and the eyes should not jerk when looking straight ahead at the stimulus. Unequal pupil size would indicate a possible serious head injury or other medical condition. Resting nystagmus may indicate a serious medical condition or the ingestion of other drugs—e.g., dissociative anesthetics like phencyclidine (PCP).

Step V: Check for Equal Tracking

Both eyes should track equally across the field of view.

Step VI: Lack of Smooth Pursuit

Check the suspect's left eye by moving the stimulus to the officer's right. Move the stimulus smoothly, at a speed that requires approximately two seconds to bring the suspect's eye as far to the side as it can go. While moving the stimulus, the officer looks at the suspect's eye and determines whether it is able to pursue the stimulus smoothly. Now, move the stimulus all the way to the officer's left, back across the suspect's field of view checking to see whether the right eye pursues smoothly. Movement of the stimulus should take approximately four seconds from the suspect's left to the suspect's right. Repeat the procedure, checking both eyes twice.

Step VII: Distinct and Sustained Nystagmus at Maximum Deviation

After you have checked both eyes for lack of smooth pursuit, check the eyes for distinct nystagmus at maximum deviation, beginning with the suspect's left eye. Simply move the stimulus to the suspect's left side until the eye has gone as far to the side as possible. Usually, no white will be showing in the corner of the eye at maximum deviation. Hold the eye at that position for a minimum of four seconds, and observe the eye for distinct and sustained nystagmus. Move the stimulus all the way across the suspect's field of view to check the right eye, holding that position for a minimum of four seconds. Repeat the procedure, checking both eyes twice.

Step VIII: Onset of Nystagmus Prior to Forty-five Degrees

Next, check for onset of nystagmus prior to forty-five degrees. Start moving the stimulus toward the right (suspect's left eye) at a speed that would take approximately four seconds for the stimulus to reach the edge of the suspect's shoulder. Watch the eye carefully for any sign of jerking. When you see it, stop and hold the stimulus and verify that the jerking continues. If the jerking continues, determine the approximate angle of onset. Now, move the stimulus to the left (suspect's right eye) at a speed that would take approximately four seconds for the stimulus to reach the edge of the suspect's shoulder. Watch the eye carefully for any sign of jerking. When you see it, stop and hold the stimulus and verify the jerking continues. Repeat the procedure, checking both eyes twice. It is important to use the full four seconds when checking the onset of nystagmus. If you move the stimulus too fast, you may miss the first sign of jerking or go past the point of onset.

Step IX: Total the Clues

Maximum number of clues possible for each eye is three. Total maximum number of clues possible for HGN is six.

Step X: Check for Vertical Nystagmus

Position the stimulus *horizontally*, approximately twelve to fifteen inches in front of the suspect's nose. Instruct the suspect to hold his or her head still, and follow the stimulus with eyes only (not raising head). Raise the stimulus until the suspect's eyes are elevated as far as possible. Hold for approximately four seconds. Watch the eyes closely for jerking as they are held at maximum elevation. For vertical nystagmus (VN) to be recorded, it must be distinct and sustained for a minimum of four seconds at maximum deviation. Vertical nystagmus may be present in subjects under the influence of high doses of alcohol (for that individual), and certain other drugs.

Walk-and-Turn

Walk-and-Turn is a field sobriety test based on the important concept of divided attention. The test requires the suspect to divide attention among mental tasks and physical tasks. The mental tasks include comprehension of verbal instructions, processing of information, and recall of memory. The physical tasks include balance and coordination; the suspect is required to maintain balance and coordination while standing still, walking, and turning. Before administering the tests, the officer should ask the suspect whether he or she has any physical problems or disabilities.

The Walk-and-Turn test has two stages—the instructions stage and the walking stage. Both stages are essential parts of the test. Important evidence of impairment often comes to light during both stages. The test requires the suspect to take nine heel-to-toe steps on a straight line, turn around in a prescribed manner, and return nine heel-to-toe steps along the line. The test should be conducted on a relatively dry, hard, level, non-slippery surface. The line should be long enough to permit the suspect to take nine heel-to-toe steps along it. If a line is not available, the officer may create a line or have a suspect walk an imaginary line.

When demonstrating the test, officers should be mindful of officer safety precautions:

- Always keep the suspect on the officer's left side when initiating demonstrations.
- Never turn your back on the suspect.
- Be aware of your surroundings (environment).
- Left-handed officers should demonstrate the test at a distance of more than arm's length for weapon retention purposes.

Walk-and-Turn instructions:

1. For standardization purposes, instruct the suspect to place the left foot on the line first (demonstrate).

2. Then instruct the suspect to place the right foot on the line, ahead of the left foot, with the heel of the right foot against the toe of the left (demonstrate).
3. Instruct the suspect to hold the arms down at the sides (demonstrate).
4. Tell the suspect to maintain that position until you have completed the instructions.
5. Inform the suspect *not* to begin walking until told to do so.
6. At this point, ask the suspect, "Do you understand?" The officer must receive some affirmative response before continuing.
7. To begin, tell the suspect to take nine heel-to-toe steps on the line (demonstrate an odd number of steps, three or five, preferably); tell the suspect on the ninth step, keep the front foot on the line, and turn by taking several small steps with the other foot (demonstrate), and return back on the line taking nine more heel-to-toe steps.
8. Tell the suspect that while walking, watch the feet at all times.
9. Tell the suspect to keep arms at the sides at all times.
10. Tell the suspect to count the steps aloud.
11. Finally, tell the suspect that once walking begins, do not stop walking until the test is completed.
12. Ask whether the suspect understands the instructions. If the suspect does not understand some part of the instructions, the officer should repeat only that part the suspect does not understand.
13. Tell the suspect to begin the test.

One-Leg Stand

One-Leg Stand is another field sobriety test that employs divided attention. The suspect's attention is divided among such simple tasks as balancing, listening, and counting aloud. Although none of these is particularly difficult in itself, the combination can be very difficult for someone who is impaired. As with the Walk-and-Turn, the officer should ask the suspect prior to administering this test whether the suspect has any physical problems or disabilities.

Like all divided attention tests, One-Leg-Stand has two stages: the instructions stage and the balance and counting stage. Both stages are important because they can affect the suspect's overall performance on the test. The test requires the suspect to stand on one leg with the other leg held out straight, approximately six inches off the ground, for thirty seconds. The test should be conducted on a reasonably hard, dry, level, and non-slippery surface. As with the Walk-and-Turn, the officer should be mindful of officer safety precautions and their surroundings (environment).

<u>One-Leg Stand instructions:</u>

1. Tell the suspect to stand with the feet together.
2. Tell the suspect to keep the arms at the sides.
3. Instruct the suspect to remain in that position until told to start.
4. Ask the suspect whether he or she understands the directions (get a verbal affirmative response).
5. Tell the suspect to raise one leg, whichever leg he or she is the most comfortable with, with the foot approximately six inches off the ground, keeping the raised foot parallel to the ground.
6. Tell the suspect to keep both legs straight, with arms at the sides.
7. Instruct the suspect to look at the elevated foot.
8. Instruct the suspect to hold that position while counting out loud in the following manner: "one thousand and one, one thousand and two, one thousand and three, and so on, until told to stop."
9. Ask the suspect whether he or she understands the directions. If the suspect does not understand some part of the instructions, the officer should repeat only that part the suspect does not understand.
10. Tell the suspect to begin the test.

Clues for SFSTs

Clues for Horizontal Gaze Nystagmus

When officers administer the HGN test, they look for three specific clues in each eye as evidence of alcohol and/or drug impairment. There are a total of six clues possible for Horizontal Gaze Nystagmus.

<u>Clue No. 1: Lack of Smooth Pursuit</u>

- Begin with the suspect's left eye.
- The first clue requires the suspect to move the eye to follow the motion of a smoothly moving stimulus. If a person is not impaired, the eyes

should move smoothly as the stimulus is moved back and forth, similar to the movement of a marble rolling across a polished pane of glass (frictionless). If the person is impaired by alcohol and/or certain other drugs, the eye should jerk noticeably as it moves back and forth, or, like a marble rolling across a sheet of course sandpaper (encountering resistance, friction).

- Check the suspect's right eye.
- Repeat the procedure for both eyes and total the clues (one point per eye).

Clue No. 2: Distinct and Sustained Nystagmus at Maximum Deviation

- Once the officer has checked for Clue No. 1, he or she will test the eyes, again beginning with the suspect's left eye, for Clue No. 2. This clue requires holding the eye at maximum deviation for four seconds and watching carefully for the jerking. If the person is impaired by alcohol and/or certain other drugs, the eye is likely to exhibit definite, distinct, and sustained jerking when held at maximum deviation for a minimum of four seconds. To score this clue as evidence of impairment, the nystagmus must be distinct and sustained for a minimum of four seconds.
- Check the suspect's right eye and observe carefully for the clue.
- Repeat the procedure for both eyes and total the clues (one point per eye).

Clue No. 3: Onset of Nystagmus Prior to 45 Degrees

The angle of onset of nystagmus is simply the point at which the eye is first seen jerking. For example, in someone at a very high BAC (0.20+), the jerking might begin almost immediately after the eye starts to move toward the side. For someone at 0.08 BAC, the jerking might not start until the eye has moved nearly to the forty-five-degree angle. Generally, the higher the BAC, the sooner the jerking will start as the eye moves toward the side. If the jerking begins prior to forty-five degrees, that person's BAC could be 0.08 or above, or the person may have ingested certain other drugs, or they may have ingested both alcohol and certain other drugs.

It is not difficult to determine when the eye has reached the forty-five-degree point, but it does require some practice on the part of the officer. If you start with the stimulus approximately twelve to fifteen inches directly in front of the nose, you will reach forty-five degrees when you have moved the stimulus an equal distance, approximately twelve to fifteen inches, to the side. Two other important indicators can be used to determine whether the eye is within forty-five degrees: at forty-five degrees, some white usually will still be visible in the corner of the eye (for most people), and if you started with the stimulus approximately twelve to fifteen inches in front of the suspect, when you reach forty-five degrees, the stimulus will usually be lined up with, or slightly beyond, the edge of the suspect's shoulder.

- Begin with the suspect's left eye.
- Slowly move the stimulus at a speed that would take approximately four seconds for the stimulus to reach the edge of the suspect's shoulder.
- As you are slowly moving the stimulus, watch the eye carefully for any sign of jerking.
- When you see the jerking begin, immediately stop moving the stimulus, hold it steady at that position, carefully observe the eye, and verify that the jerking continues. If the officer actually has found the point of onset, the eye will continue to jerk when the stimulus is held steady. Score the clue if the jerking continues. If not, continue on slowly until the forty-five-degree position is reached.
- Check the suspect's right eye and observe carefully for the clue.
- Repeat the procedure for both eyes and total the clues (one point per eye).

Based on the original developmental research into Horizontal Gaze Nystagmus, the criterion for this test is four. If a person exhibits at least four out of a possible six clues, the implication is a BAC of above 0.10; however, more recent studies indicate that HGN can provide valid indications to support arrest decisions at 0.08 BAC. Using this criterion, the test is 77 percent accurate.

Clues for Vertical Gaze Nystagmus

Although vertical nystagmus was not examined in the original research that led to the validation of the SFST battery, it can be used by the officer to determine whether the suspect may have a high dose (for that individual) of alcohol and/or other drugs. Procedures are outlined above for the proper administration of the vertical nystagmus test. If the person has a high dose (for that individual) of alcohol and/or certain other drugs, the eyes will jerk *vertically* as the eyes are elevated as far as possible for approximately four seconds. The jerking will be distinct and sustained.

This clue is not scored like the other tests. This clue is either *present* or *not present*, as it is used as observational only. If the clue is present, the officer may conclude the suspect has a high dose (for that individual) of alcohol and/or other drugs.

Clues for Walk-and-Turn

When administering the Walk-and-Turn test, we look for certain specific behaviors at certain times in the test. Each behavior, or action, is considered as one clue. There is a maximum of eight clues on this test.

The first two clues are checked during the instruction stage:

- Cannot balance during instructions: This clue is recorded only if the feet actually break apart. During the instructions stage, the officer does not record the clue simply because the suspect raises arms or wobbles slightly.
- Starts too soon: This clue cannot be recorded unless the suspect was told not to start walking until directed to do so.

Each of these first two clues, like all clues that follow in this test, can be accumulated only once.

The next four clues are checked while the suspect is walking, either up or down the line.

- Stops while walking (pauses to regain balance): It is because of this clue that it is important for the officer to inform the suspect *not* to stop walking once the test begins.

- Misses heel-to-toe: A gap of at least one-half inch is necessary to record this clue.

- Steps off the line.

- Uses arms to balance: A movement of the arms of six or more inches from the side is required to record this clue.

- Improper turn: This clue should be recorded if the suspect loses balance on turn (staggers, stumbles, etc.) or turns other than the way the officer demonstrated.

- Incorrect number of steps: It is the number of steps that the suspect physically takes that matters in this clue. Mistakes in the verbal count do not justify recording this clue.

The Walk-and-Turn test may be terminated by the officer if the suspect cannot safely complete it. For example:

- Suspect steps off the line three or more times.
- Suspect nearly falls.
- Suspect gets into a "leg-lock" position (legs crossed, unable to move).

Based on the original developmental research into the Walk-and-Turn test, the criterion for this test is two. If a person exhibits at least two out of a possible eight clues, the implication is that the suspect has a BAC above 0.10. Using that criterion, this test is 68 percent accurate. There are restrictions to this test: the original research indicated that individuals over sixty-five years of age had difficulty performing this test.

Combining the Clues of the Horizontal Gaze Nystagmus and Walk-and-Turn

Based on the original research, officers will be 80 percent accurate in classifying suspects who are above 0.10 BAC. With a combination of four or more clues of HGN and two or more clues of the Walk-and-Turn, suspects can be correctly classified as above 0.10 BAC 80 percent of the time.

Clues for the One-Leg Stand

When administering the One-Leg Stand test, officers look for certain specific behaviors. Each behavior or action is considered one clue.

There are a maximum number of four clues on this test:

- Swaying: Swaying means a distinct, noticeable side-to-side or front-to-back movement of the elevated foot or of the suspect's body.
- Using the arms for balance: A movement of the arms of six inches or more from the side is sufficient to record this clue.
- Hopping
- Putting the foot down: If the suspect's foot touches the ground before 30 seconds elapse, have the suspect raise it and continue counting from where he or she left off until told to stop.

The One-Leg Stand test may be terminated by the officer if the suspect cannot safely complete it. For example:

- If the suspect puts the foot down three or more times before thirty seconds elapse.
- If the suspect nearly falls.

Based on the original developmental research for the One-Leg Stand test, the criterion for this test is two. If the person exhibits at least two out of the possible four clues, the implication is that the suspect's BAC is above 0.10. Using that criterion, this test is 65 percent accurate.

There are restrictions to this test: the original research indicated individuals over sixty-five years of age or fifty pounds or more overweight had difficulty performing this test.

The evidence gathered during the detection process is vital to establish the elements of the violation and to support subsequent prosecution of the offense. This evidence is observational in nature, and therefore is extremely short-lived. Officers must be able to recognize and act on their own observations. But officers also must be able to recall those observations and describe them clearly and convincingly to secure a conviction. The officer is inundated with considerable evidence of DUI: sights, sounds, smells, etc. The officer recognizes this evidence, sometimes subconsciously, and bases any subsequent arrest decision on it. However, later the officer must be able to recollect this observational evidence and be able to express the evidence clearly in any written report or oral testimony.

Officers need a system for documenting their observations in notes at the scene of DUI investigations. To facilitate note-taking at the scene, there is a standard DWI investigation field note. Each section of the form is broken down, and officers are thoroughly trained in the types of notes to be taken in each section.

In addition to the note-taking guide, maintaining the "SFST field arrest log" is mandatory and extremely important for the officer. The SFST field arrest log is used to record the results of the SFSTs performed on *all* suspected impaired subjects. This log is extremely important in documenting an officer's experience and proficiency in performing and interpreting SFSTs. Officers should always transfer their documentation from the note-taking guide to the log.

Most state laws dictate the type of specimen(s) law enforcement can collect as corroborative evidence in a potential DUI case. For alcohol-only DUI cases, blood and breath are the specimens of choice, with blood being the gold standard, and breath being the least-intrusive and easiest to obtain. For drug-impaired driving cases, or alcohol- and drug-suspected combinations, blood, breath, and urine are the current specimens of choice, with blood being the gold standard, and breath (for alcohol only) and urine (for the drugs) being the least-intrusive and easiest to obtain. Oral fluid or saliva testing for drugs, for the most part, mimics that of blood. The only exception is THC (cannabis). Oral fluid will likely detect THC from ingestion up to a maximum period of eighteen to twenty-four hours, versus blood, which can detect up to twelve days.

All methods of alcohol and drug testing have their own benefits, as well as limitations. Hence, the choice of test depends entirely upon the confines of statutory limits, availability of analytical instrumentation and personnel within the geographic area the officer is assigned, and budget restraints.

Understanding Alcohol as a Drug

I firmly believe the most common misperceptions about DUI situations are the public's concerns and the age-old myth, "two beers/drinks, and you're drunk!" The inevitable fallout from this myth from the law enforcement perspective is the hesitancy of people to trust, and ultimately submit to, the subsequent required chemical test, most specifically the breath alcohol test. A rather elemental education in the clinical effects of alcohol is in order to debunk this myth.

Alcohol is a very small molecule. It has a chemical makeup of CH3 CH2 OH. As a pure chemical, it is odorless, colorless, and tasteless; it does, however, produce a burning sensation in the mouth and mixes freely with water. It is available only in liquid form. Because it also has a caloric value, it is considered a food source.

There are primarily three types of alcohol:

- Isopropyl alcohol (rubbing alcohol)
- Methyl alcohol or wood alcohol (cleaning agents—this is poisonous)
- Ethyl alcohol or ethanol (the primary constituent of alcoholic beverages)

Ethyl alcohol, or ethanol, is generally harmless when consumed in moderate quantities. However, when consumed in sufficiently large quantities, it can be lethal. Its effect on the body is that of a central nervous system (CNS) depressant, or an anesthetic. *Alcohol is always a CNS depressant*—it is never a stimulant. Many people think it is a stimulant because its first noticeable effect is to reduce inhibitions and promote a feeling of well-being.

Ethyl alcohol is produced by the fermentation of such organic substances as fruit, fruit juices, malt, cereal grain extract, vegetable pulp, molasses, or other plant-grown properties. The maximum natural alcoholic content of fermented beverage is 14 percent to 15 percent by volume. Examples of these types of fermented beverages are beers, ales, porters, and wines.

Distilled beverages, such as whiskey, vodka, gin, and rum are produced by heating fermented alcohol mixtures. Since alcohol boils at a lower temperature than water, the alcohol can be boiled off or distilled, thereby increasing the alcoholic content of the finished beverage.

In addition to alcohol and water, alcoholic beverages contain numerous compounds or impurities known as "congeners." Congeners typically impart a characteristic flavor and odor to the beverage and give rise to what people call the smell of alcohol or beer on a person's breath. These congeners constitute a very small portion of the total volume of an alcoholic beverage.

The proof number of a beverage represents about twice the percent of alcohol by volume. For example, 100 proof whiskeys contain 50 percent alcohol by volume. Most alcoholic beverages have a maximum of approximately 50 percent alcohol by volume, or 100 proof. The remainder is water and congeners. Beer has a relatively low alcoholic content and is approximately 90 percent water.

Alcohol can be absorbed through the lining of the mouth. Such absorption is normally insignificant, since the fluid typically leaves the mouth rapidly. The presence of alcohol persists in the mouth after the alcohol has been swallowed. However, the mouth of a person will be free of alcohol after about ten minutes since the alcohol was last present in the mouth.

About 25 percent of the alcohol is absorbed directly into the bloodstream unchanged, through the stomach wall. The exact amount is variable and influenced by the emptying time of the stomach. No other substances, not even liquids, are absorbed from the stomach. The remainder of alcohol is absorbed from the small intestine. Very little alcohol gets past the first eight to ten inches of the small intestine. The alcohol then travels via the portal vein to the liver. Thereafter, it travels via the circulatory system to the heart, lungs, and back to the heart, where it is then pumped to all parts of the body. Since alcohol is hydrophilic and is therefore present in any body tissue or fluid as a function of the water content of that tissue or fluid, organs such as the brain, liver, and kidneys, which have a large blood supply (blood has a high water content), initially receive a considerable amount of the circulating blood containing alcohol.

Alcohol first affects the parts of the brain that control a person's judgment, morals, and powers of attention. As a result, one's self-confidence has a greater tendency to increase; hence, risk-taking increases. The next human defenses to go are emotional control and then motor coordination. Finally, if alcohol is consumed in sufficient quantities, functioning of the oldest part of the brain that automatically controls a person's body functions can become impaired, so that people can lose complete control of themselves, pass into a coma, and ultimately die, if the respiratory center of the brain is sufficiently depressed. This condition is known as alcohol poisoning. Alcohol poisoning can occur at BACs of approximately 0.50 percent and above.

Between the mild effects and the severe effects of alcohol, there is a progressive deterioration in performance:

- Speech becomes slurred.
- Vision becomes impaired.
  - The pupils of the eye can enlarge, and reaction to visual stimuli becomes slower; bright lights and glare are bothersome (if you doubt this, check the lighting in the next bar or tavern of your choice; you will notice dimmed lighting, not bright lights. Bright lighting inhibits consumption.)
  - Distance judgment is impaired, as well as the ability to see things to one side or the other of the visual field (peripheral vision).
  - The ability to focus from near to far objects decreases at BACs of about 0.06 percent.
  - At higher BACs—those of 0.10 percent or higher—blurred vision can occur.
- Reaction time increases, and physical coordination is impaired.
  - The beginning of impairment of physical coordination can be with a BAC as low as 0.02 percent.
  - Motor coordination tasks that require discrimination (like driving or operating machinery) are impaired at BACs as low as 0.05 percent.

There is no evidence alcohol improves circulation. Following absorption, blood alcohol dilates the vessels of the skin and permits an increase in skin blood flow. This accounts for the flushed face of some drinkers.

Alcohol stimulates the kidneys to produce urine. Moderate use of alcohol does not appear to cause any kidney damage. Heavy use of alcohol causes an accumulation of fat in the liver. This can, over an extended period of time, result in an inflammation of the liver, commonly called *cirrhosis*.

When absorption and distribution are complete, alcohol is distributed to areas of the body proportional with their fluid/water content. The rate of absorption varies somewhat from person to person and for the same person at different times. Alcohol begins to pass into the bloodstream within one or two minutes after consumption. More alcohol is absorbed within fifteen minutes and nearly 90 percent within one hour. In most cases, alcohol is completely absorbed within one to one-and-one-half hours; however, in some cases it may require almost three hours for total absorption.

Absorption through the stomach wall is slow and represents only a small portion of the intake. In contrast, absorption through the small intestine is rapid. Food in the stomach, especially fatty foods taken both immediately before and during the intake of alcoholic beverages, delays the absorption by holding the alcohol in the stomach. Food taken a couple of hours prior to drinking, especially sweet foods, may actually accelerate the absorption rate. There is a small valve at the bottom of the stomach called the pyloric sphincter. The sphincter opens and closes, allowing the contents of the stomach to empty into the small intestine. If that valve is open, the alcohol will go directly into the small intestine, thus rapidly accelerating the absorption time.

Alcohol is eliminated from the body by a biochemical reaction and direct excretion. Between 90 percent and 98 percent of the alcohol in the body is burned up, or oxidized, to carbon dioxide and water in the liver. A small amount, 2 percent to 8 percent, is excreted unchanged, through the breath, urine, tears, saliva, and perspiration. The average rate of elimination is reported at being 0.015 percent per hour. At relatively low BACs, the average rate is only about 0.01 percent per hour. Quantitated: a man weighing 150 pounds eliminates about two-thirds of an ounce of 100 proof whiskey per hour. This rate of elimination is not affected by stimulants (drugs or coffee), or even exercise.

For the purposes of discussion, the amount of alcohol in the body, or more specifically in the blood, is termed blood alcohol concentration, or BAC. BAC is expressed in weight of alcohol per volume of blood. More specifically, it is the number of grams of alcohol that are found in every 100 milliliters of a person's blood. BACs are fractions of one percent concentration. The so-called illegal limit of BAC in all states is 0.08 percent. If a person has a BAC of 0.08 percent, it means there are 0.08 grams of ethanol, or ethyl alcohol, in every 100 milliliters of his or her blood.

How much alcohol does a person have to drink to reach a BAC of 0.08 percent? Take an average male weighing 175 pounds and in reasonably good physical condition. Assume he does his drinking on an empty stomach. It is estimated that person would have to consume four cans of beer, four glasses of wine, or four shots of 80 proof whiskey in a fairly short time period, one hour or less, to reach a BAC of 0.08 percent. There are numerous physiological variables that can affect BAC, such as gender, weight, stomach contents, medical/health condition, and metabolic rate. However, I submit that four drinks per hour, over the course of an evening averaging three to four hours—i.e., twelve to sixteen drinks—is not social drinking, but hard drinking—the kind that makes that person a universal threat to the motoring public.

Long answer on paper, but a short explanation to absorption, distribution, and elimination of alcohol from the human body. Myth debunked.

Courts and Convictions

The vast majority of our nation's prosecutor's offices are significantly under-funded and -resourced. Consequently, most offices provide only minimal training to the young attorneys who handle misdemeanor DWI and DUI cases. Many of these prosecutors are ill-equipped to overcome the bevy of experienced defense lawyers and expert witnesses they face regularly. Indeed, one of the most common reasons that DWI/DUI drivers escape justice is the lack of adequate prosecutor training.

In an effort to overcome this deficit, it is strongly suggested that prosecutors develop a working partnership with their professional peers at The American Prosecutors Research Institute's National Traffic Law Center (NTLC). The mission of the NTLC is to improve the quality of justice in traffic safety adjudications by increasing the awareness of highway safety issues through the compilation, creation, and dissemination of legal and technical information, and by providing training and reference services.

When prosecutors deal with challenges to the use of breath-testing instruments, blood tests, horizontal gaze nystagmus, crash reconstruction, and other evidence, the NTLC can assist with technical and case law research. Likewise, when faced with inquiries from community groups about getting impaired drivers off the road, NTLC can provide research and statistics concerning the effectiveness of administrative license revocation, ignition interlock systems, sobriety checkpoints, and much more.

NTLC has a clearinghouse of resources, including case law, legislation, research studies, training materials, trial documents, and a directory of professionals who work in the fields of crash reconstruction, toxicology, drug recognition, and many others. The information catalogued by the center covers a wide range of topics, with particular emphasis on impaired driving and vehicular homicide issues.

The professional staff at NTLC includes experienced trial attorneys and research staff. Assistance is specifically provided in all areas of trial preparation, including methods to counter specific defenses. NTLC facilitates the direct exchange of information among prosecutors, judges, and other criminal justice professionals in the field to prevent duplication of effort.

NTLC was created in cooperation with the NHTSA and works closely with NHTSA and the National Association of Prosecutor Coordinators to develop and deliver prosecutor training programs, such as:

- Prosecution of Driving While Under the Influence
- Prosecuting the Drugged Driver
- Lethal Weapon: DUI Homicide
- Protecting Lives/Saving Futures

Each course incorporates substantive legal presentations by faculty with skill-building sessions where participants take part in a mock trial. The participants are critiqued and videotaped to assist in improving their trial skills.

NTLC is a program of the American Prosecutors Research Institute (APRI), the nonprofit affiliate of the National District Attorneys Association. APRI's principal function is to enhance prosecution in America by providing training, technical assistance, and research to support local prosecutors.

In addition to the training programs of the NTLC, twenty-eight states, with the support and assistance from the NHTSA, have promulgated and promoted the development and expansion of a Traffic Safety Resource Prosecutor (TSRP). TSRPs fill a critical void as the in-state experts on traffic-related offenses, including impaired driving and vehicular homicides. TSRPs understand the nuances of their state statutes and case law, building relationships with each of their state's prosecutor's offices and forge solid interactions with state highway safety offices. TSRPs provide state-specific training and technical assistance, while being part of a national network of traffic experts to assist with new challenges as they arise. TSRPs are essential to effective traffic safety adjudications. TSRPs:

- Serve as their respective state's experts on DWI/DUI law and evidence
- Provide continuing professional education on pertinent issues, including trial advocacy, visual trial techniques, and complex defense challenges
- Research and provide assistance on traffic safety issues (many TSRPs publish trial manuals, predicate questions, memoranda of law, and legal updates to keep their prosecutors current about the state of the law)
- Assist, or "second chair," trial prosecutors on complex motions, hearings, and trials.

TSRPs can also serve the traffic safety community and promote public understanding by:

- Providing much-needed leadership on a statewide basis
- Training law enforcement officers on how to prepare their cases and testify in court
- Creating and distributing educational materials for public consumption (many TSRPs publish quarterly newsletters or engage in other outreach activities)
- Serving as liaisons between prosecutors and the traffic safety community

The NTLC and the TSRPs are invaluable resources to local prosecutors' offices, and each can certainly assist in training and resource/research material to offset any financial handicap.

Case preparation begins with the officer's first contact with the suspect. The officer begins by utilizing field notes to document all the observations of the defendant at the scene and all evidence gathered during the each phase of the contact. The officer's notes on observations made at the scene are critical, as the defendant will not look or act the same in court as he or she did at the time of the incident. Each action, behavior, statement, and observation made of the defendant by the officer can subsequently be used by the prosecution to show intoxication. Provided the officer accurately documents those actions, behaviors, statements, and observations on the field notes and translates those notes into a clear and convincing narrative report, the officer can then review the narrative report and the field notes to adequately prepare for trial.

Upon receipt of a subpoena or trial notification, the officer should:

1. Review all records and reports associated with the case:
   - DWI Investigation Field Notes
   - SFST Field Arrest Log
   - Narrative report
   - Chemical test(s)
   - Videotape or photographs, if available/applicable
   - Other
2. Revisit the scene, if possible.
3. Review all evidence and the officer's opinion.

4. Meet with the prosecutor, if possible, and ask any questions you may have regarding your testimony.
5. Review possible tactics the prosecutor expects the defense to use.
6. Review the officer's résumé and credentials.
7. Try to get copies of transcripts of previous trials to review your strong and weak points.

Successful DUI prosecution also depends on the clarity and completeness with which an officer's observations are presented. The officer must be able to convey observations with sufficient clarity to convince others there was probable cause to believe the suspect was under the influence. Chemical test evidence may be suppressed if the officer does not adequately establish there were reasonable grounds for the arrest prior to the test.

A pretrial conference with the prosecutor assigned to the case is essential. The officer should insist in the most strenuous terms on a pretrial conference, if at all possible. This conference will enable the prosecutor to develop the officer's testimony and bring out the most important facts necessary. The prosecutor needs an opportunity not only to review the evidence, but also to discuss case strategy.

During the pretrial conference, the officer should be honest and forthright to avoid any possibility of surprises during the trial. Together with the prosecutor, the officer should review all evidence and the reason for his or her conclusions to arrest. Weak and strong points in the case should be brought to the attention of the prosecutor. In addition, the officer should ask the prosecutor to review the trial tactics and evidence to be presented:

*   The officer's training and experience
*   The narrative arrest report
*   The officer's ability to articulate observations
*   Any documents or physical evidence to be presented at the trial
*   Questions the prosecutor will ask the officer
*   Any anticipated defense tactics
*   Possible responses to defense arguments and questions
*   The defendant's driving record

The main point of the pretrial conference is to familiarize the prosecutor with the case and the officer's qualifications as a witness, as well as to review case strategy. If a pretrial conference cannot be scheduled, the officer should try to identify the main points to be discussed with the prosecutor in the few minutes they will have just before the trial.

Guidelines for Direct Testimony

The officer's basic job is to prove the suspect was impaired by alcohol and/or other drugs. The following are basic guidelines for the officer to follow:

- Tell the truth. Honesty is always the best policy. Telling the truth requires that a witness testify accurately as to what he or she knows.
- Read your report before you come to court. Go over the details in your mind so you will have an independent recollection of the events of the arrest.
- Dress neatly and professionally. If the department uniform is not worn, wear a coat and tie. Leave sunglasses and extraneous, cumbersome equipment in your car before coming into the courtroom.
- Look at the jury when testifying. If the trial is a bench trial, look at the judge. Even when the defense attorney asking the question is not standing near the box, always talk to the jury or the judge and maintain eye contact with them.
- Do not be afraid to say, "I do not know" or "I do not remember."
- Take your time. Do not feel pressured to give a quick answer. After a question is asked, there may be an objection; allow this to happen. Likewise, when you hear the word "objection," stop testifying.
- Answer the question that is asked and then stop. Do not volunteer information not asked for, or you will risk causing a mistrial, or even an immediate acquittal.
- Avoid contact with the defense attorney prior to trial and during breaks.
- Do not be upset if the prosecutor and the defense attorney appear friendly to each other. Both have specific roles to play in the case, but that does not preclude a personal or professional relationship.

- Juries often focus on an officer's demeanor more than content of testimony. The officer should be polite and courteous during testimony and should not become agitated because of defense questions. Do not take personal issue with defense statements (stick to the facts).

- Do not bring manuals or articles into court for reference. Any review of these materials should have occurred before court.

- Explain technical terms in layman's language. For example, "Nystagmus means an involuntary jerking of the eyes."

- Pay attention to what evidence/testimony can be and is excluded. If the officer testifies on subject matter that was excluded, it could result in a mistrial.

- When describing the suspect's performance on the SFSTs, state the suspect "performed the test as demonstrated" or "did not perform the test as demonstrated." Provide specific descriptive details concerning exactly what the suspect did or failed to do on the test (e.g., "stepped off the line twice and staggered while turning").

- Do not appear biased against the defendant. Testify accurately and completely, but also dispassionately. The officer should not embellish the testimony.

Typical Defense Tactics

The defense relies on several factors to impeach or discredit the officer's testimony. In an attempt to impeach or discredit the officer, the defense will try to do the following:

- Establish inconsistencies
- Bring up testimony that is at odds with other established experts or procedures
  - The officer should do his or her homework and review the relevant literature.
- Highlight lack of recall
  - Try to be prepared, but do not be afraid to say, "I do not know." Be honest.

The defense will also try to expose the court to alternative conditions that account for your observations—for example, sickness, injury, or existing medical condition of the defendant. The defense will also challenge the officer's credentials by claiming a bona fide expert has both formal training resulting in a high degree of knowledge and experience in applying that knowledge. The defense will do this by directly challenging the officer's formal training and experience and by demonstrating the officer's lack of knowledge in the field by contrasting the officer's knowledge with a defense expert's knowledge.

Last, the defense will attempt to demonstrate the officer did not follow testing procedures established by departmental policy, training, or legal precedent. If the officer follows the administration protocols established and taught during his or her training and administered each test by the book every time tests are conducted, this tactic will not be successful.

Lieutenant Colonel Darrell E. Fisher is a thirty-two-year law enforcement veteran in Nebraska, spending nearly four years as a deputy sheriff in Buffalo County, Kearney, Nebraska, and the past twenty-eight-plus years with the Nebraska State Patrol.

Before achieving his current rank, Lt. Col. Fisher served as the troop commander in Headquarters Troop, Lincoln, Nebraska, for five years. Lt. Col. Fisher graduated from the Nebraska State Patrol Training Academy in 1979 and served his first duty station assignment with the Uniformed Traffic Services Division, Headquarters Troop, in Lincoln. He worked numerous assignments in traffic, including nine years on the Special Weapons and Tactics Team (SWAT) and six years on the Selective Traffic Enforcement Program, as well as serving in Executive and Dignitary Protection, and as a field training officer.

Promoted to sergeant in the Training Academy in 1987, Lt. Col. Fisher rose to lieutenant in 1994 and served as commander of the Academy and the director of training for the Nebraska State Patrol. He laterally transferred back to Traffic Services in 1999 and was promoted to Troop Commander in 2000.

Lt. Col. Fisher holds a Bachelor of Science degree from the University of Nebraska at Kearney with a comprehensive major in criminal justice, graduating in 1979. In addition, he is a graduate of the Northwestern University Center for Public Safety School of Police Staff and Command.

Lt. Col. Fisher is certified as an instructor in the Standardized Field Sobriety Test battery. In addition, he is a certified drug recognition expert (DRE), as well as a certified DRE instructor. He teaches extensively in Nebraska and across the United States.

Lt. Col. Fisher holds an at-large position on the Technical Advisory Panel, a subcommittee of the International Association of Chiefs of Police (IACP) Highway Safety Committee, which provides information and advice as requested concerning the Drug Evaluation and Classification Program, Standardized Field Sobriety Testing, and areas of concern dealing with impaired driving. In addition, he is a past vice chair and chairperson for the IACP DRE Section. The IACP DRE Section serves as the coordinating body among the various DRE associations or chapters within the states and serves as a resource to respond to the views and needs of the membership.

Lt. Col. Fisher is recognized in several jurisdictions as an expert witness in the area of drunken and drugged driving and is listed as such in the National Resource Directory for the National Traffic Law Center, a section of the National District Attorneys Association in Alexandria, Virginia. By his association with the directory, Lt. Col. Fisher has been selected on two occasions to serve on the faculty of the Prosecuting the Drugged Driver course, held at the National Advocacy Center in Columbia, South Carolina.

Lt. Col. Fisher was promoted to his current position as assistant superintendent of the Nebraska State Patrol in 2005.

Dedication: *My contribution to this book is dedicated first to my wife, Debra, and my daughters, Erin and Shannon. Their sacrifice and patience with me throughout these many years have allowed me the time to teach others much of what is contained in this chapter. They are my inspiration, and I am thankful for the forgiveness they have shown me through the ups and downs of my roles as a husband, a father, and a Nebraska State Trooper. You three are the greatest!*

My contributions to this book are also dedicated to the thousands of law enforcement professionals—past, present, and future—who have chosen or will choose the wonderful career of troopers, deputy sheriffs, and police officers; who toil daily on the road, putting their lives in harm's way to detect and apprehend one of the biggest killers on our roadways—the impaired driver. May this book be a small form of assistance in helping them to better serve the public.

Preparing Officers for DUI Testing, Investigations, and Testimony

Daniel W. Lonsdorf

Patrol Major

Wisconsin State Patrol

Highway Safety Director

Bureau of Transportation Safety

ASPATORE

Suspicion and Testing

The type of training officers receive on DUI (driving under the influence) procedures depends on the department. It can vary from a few hours to more than a week. On-road (field) training can be an essential component of officer training, especially in drunken driving detection and arrest. The topics covered typically address the effects of alcohol on the body, how fast it's absorbed, etc. These are done by lecture. Then officers learn what to look for in driver behavior that might be indicative of impairment. Often these will include videos of actual traffic stop cases, or staged videos set up as training tools.

Officers learn to notice typical signs of impaired driving, such as weaving, abrupt stops and starts, and delayed reactions. Next, officers learn about observational clues to look for when they approach the driver inside the car. These are both lecture and video. Officers are taught to use all their senses to see, smell, and hear the typical signs of impairment. These include the odor of intoxicants, slurred speech, bloodshot and red eyes, flushed face, confusion with their surroundings, etc. Lectures will further teach officers to ask specific questions about the driver's history that day, such as how much they had to drink, where, what kind, starting when, stopping when, time of last drink, food to eat, approximate current time, date, day of the week, and location. Having the driver recite the alphabet is a great way to test for impairment, alertness, and slurred speech.

After lectures; officers then perform repeated trials of field tests on both sober and actual dosed volunteers under controlled labs with variable known blood alcohol levels to get comfortable in administering the tests, interpretation of the results, and witnessing the differing levels of performance at increasing levels of alcohol intake. This portion of the training is by far the most valuable to officers because they actually perform standard field sobriety tests on real people, many of whom are impaired by known levels of alcohol.

Much of the training from this point will focus on the arrest, the handling of the suspect, the paperwork and forms, and then the evidentiary test of the arrested person. This is often covered by lecture as the actual forms are presented, and in some cases, the officers actually complete mock versions to become comfortable with their content. In many police agencies, the training can include the certification to operate a breath-testing device as part of the curriculum. This provides officers valuable insight in how the machines operate and those details they need to watch for so as not to void the test results. This portion of the training generally includes officers learning on the actual breath-testing device in use at their department and in most cases, will include actual dosed volunteers.

Once officers have a better understanding of the process and how evidence is obtained in a drunken driving case, they are lectured on report writing, courtroom preparation, and testimony. Someone often presents this from the legal profession, where available. This may be a local or state prosecutor, judge, or even a defense lawyer in some cases. It is critical to emphasize that after all the formalized training, most new officers enter a field training stage and work closely with a more experienced officer. It is here where much of their practical application of traffic enforcement is engrained and where the processing of drunken driving arrests becomes much clearer.

Retraining for new procedures is generally handled at an annual in-service training session common with most police agencies. Often, the deployment of new equipment is delivered during the course of annual training, but not exclusively. With new equipment comes new training. Police agencies emphasize training to officers as a matter of routine. When the equipment involves breath-testing devices, a certification is generally required to operate the machine. Certification requires training, or at least a demonstration of competence to successfully operate the device. If a new equipment item is deployed outside of the annual training, special training sessions may be held to get officers familiar with the new item and how it works.

Suspicions of someone driving under the influence can be raised from several venues. Routine patrol observations will be different from observations made of an individual involved in a crash, or one being treated at a hospital for injuries, possibly because of a crash.

When officers observe traffic, there are telltale signs of impairment. Weaving about the traffic lane or even across the lanes and onto the shoulder are common observations. This clue is indicative of a distracted driver, which is what an impaired driver is. Officers see weaving in increasing frequency as more drivers find new ways to become distracted inside their cars. The most common distractions include cell phone dialing, checking cell phone voice mail, searching for contact numbers, text messaging, reading, arguing, eating, adjusting the stereo, programming a GPS (global positioning system), performing personal hygiene, and being overly tired.

All of these are distracting and cause drivers to weave about their lanes and, at times, across the lanes into other lanes and onto the shoulder. All of these behaviors are dangerous and similar in how they appear to observing police officers, with one exception. Drivers impaired by alcohol tend to respond more slowly to the drifting of their vehicle than do other distracted drivers. In addition, alcohol-impaired drivers tend to overcorrect when attempting to compensate for their actions.

There are generally several ways officers observe impaired driving, such as through routine patrol, following a crash, or while investigating the circumstances of a crash at a hospital. During routine patrol, an officer's attention is quickly drawn to some form of unusual driving behavior, such as weaving, driving too slow or too fast, abrupt starts and stops, and no headlights. Excellent patrol officers, specifically tuned into detecting impaired drivers, are often taught to be the follower, rather than the leader, when it comes to observing driver behavior. When waiting at a stop sign or light, officers should wait for an approaching car to pass by them first, rather than pull out in front of it. This way they can follow and make observations about its driving from behind. Often, the impaired or suspicious driver will become nervous about the officer following them and quickly turn down some side street. These are excellent indicators of suspicious activity and should raise an officer's awareness for further observations.

Upon approach to a vehicle, the odor is always the first sign of a problem. Some impaired drivers can hide it better than others, but not many. What they do not realize is how strong the odor builds inside an enclosed automobile right before they roll the window down for the officer. This is especially evident in colder weather. Some more clever drivers will quickly get out of the car to meet the officer halfway. This helps to mask the odor and hide the possibility of open intoxicants inside the car, but is a telltale sign to the officer of someone attempting to conceal a problem. By getting out of the car, the driver often demonstrates early signs of impairment by their walk, their demeanor, and their standing.

On the mental checklist of behaviors or signs of impairment, first is odor, then balance, along with speech. These are the primary clues. Through preliminary questioning, an officer gets the suspect to talk, thereby projecting an odor (if any) and providing speech. Slurred speech is another telltale sign of impairment. The suspect's eyes are often bloodshot and glassy. Officers generally ask the suspect a series of orientation questions to gain a sense of their awareness and the degree of impairment. Questions may include things such as the approximate time, date or day, approximate location, where they are going, where they are coming from, and even about how much they have had to drink.

Post-crash interviews may need to be handled much differently from roadside interviews because of the person's injuries. Of the questions noted above, these can vary depending on the officer and the answers. As an example, most suspects will give the officer the standard "two drinks" when answering how many they had. This may be a starting point for the officer to ask questions about how long ago the last drink was, where they had it, when they started drinking, what they were drinking, etc. I once had a person give some thought to the question of how much he had had to drink, then paused, and told me, "It could not have been more than a case." I admired his honesty, but he was extremely impaired. Officers can also ask a series of questions regarding food intake, sleep history, etc. All these questions help set the foundation of clues officers can use to determine the level of impairment and whether the person should be taken into custody. Further, they will serve the officer and the prosecutor well in helping establish probable cause for a subsequent arrest, should the situation lead to that end.

The State Patrol uses the standard field sobriety tests of the Walk-and-Turn, the One-Leg Stand, and Horizontal Gaze Nystagmus. These three tests have generally become the standard in America for impaired driving field tests.

The Walk-and-Turn test requires the subject to walk a straight line (either imaginary or actual), heel-to-toe, nine steps forward, pivot around, and return nine steps. Officers are trained to instruct the subject on how to complete this maneuver and demonstrate it to the subject. By providing specific instructions, officers look for clues, or indicators of impairment, during the performance of the test. Deviations from the instructions by the subject are indicators. How and in which direction the subject pivots, in deviation from the instructions, are also indicators. Other clues include not walking heel-to-toe, swaying, staggering, falling, extending their arms out to the sides, quitting, losing count, not taking the proper number of steps, etc.

During the Walk-and-Turn test, officers ask the suspect to count each step. This requires divided attention. Divided attention testing has long been a significant vehicle used in the detection of impairment. By asking the subject to both walk a straight line and count, their attention is divided between two tasks at the same time. The test seems simple enough, but it becomes a difficult task when the person is not sober.

The next test is called the One-Leg Stand, where the subject is asked to simply balance on one leg with the other held straight out in front of them a few inches off the ground, arms down to their sides. They should remain in this position while counting to thirty at about one count per second. Officers demonstrate this test also. They are trained to look for clues, such as falling, swaying, losing balance, putting the foot down, losing count, and not counting. As with the first test, officers ask the subject to count while performing the balance test, creating a divided attention challenge.

The final test is rather simple to administer, but is complicated to understand in the sense of its origins. The test is called the Horizontal Gaze Nystagmus test. Officers ask the subject to stare straight ahead and then use their eyes to follow the point of an object the officer holds up and moves from side to side. The subject should not move their head, just their eyes. Officers are trained to look at the pupils of the subject's eyes for indicators of impairment.

The eyes of individuals under the influence of intoxicants provide clues to that person's impairment in three general ways. The first indicator involves the eye's inability to smoothly follow the object from side to side. In an impaired person, the eye will jerk abruptly in its attempt to follow the object. The second indicator involves having the pupil move to the far left and right edge of its vision and the officer observes the presence of pupil movement (nystagmus), or jerkiness, while holding a position at these outer edges. The third indicator involves the officer slowly moving the object to the side and watching for the onset of nystagmus (jerkiness). If the onset begins prior to the general angle of forty-five degrees from straight-ahead, the likelihood is the subject is impaired.

All three tests are usually administered unless the suspect has some physical limitations, the roadside conditions do not permit it, or it could create an undue officer-safety risk to perform them.

There is a set system of instructions and guidelines officers are trained to follow and utilize when administering these three tests. The scoring criteria are pre-determined, and the officers are trained to look for these clues. When a suspect reaches that threshold, the test can be terminated. This standard practice helps remove much of the subjectivity from sobriety tests, and the tests have been clinically proved to be the most indicative of a person's impairment. The tests are generally given by the officer who made the traffic stop and only take a couple of minutes to complete.

DUI is indicated by failure of the minimum thresholds for the three tests. As an example, the person steps off the line three times during the Walk-and-Turn test, or puts a foot down for balance three times during the One-Leg Stand.

Interpreting the variations in field test results is different for everyone because everyone is different. Some people are well-practiced at their balance, even at high levels of intoxication. Others can hardly stand, much less walk a straight line. Officers are trained to collectively observe all of the clues demonstrated by a suspect to make an interpretation as to impairment. Remember, these are made prior to arrest, as an officer is determining whether probable cause exists to make an arrest.

Field test results might vary because officers may administer them with some variations. As noted above, some people have much better balance than others do, even at higher levels of alcohol intake. The officers are not attempting to narrow down the level of alcohol, but to determine whether the person has a prohibitive minimum level of impairment. Seasoned drinkers might be quite good at standing on one leg, but their response to questions, the odor, their speech, and their eyes may still give them away.

Analysis and Investigation

Generally, once an officer determines that a person may be impaired by alcohol or another substance, they may ask the suspect to blow into a device called a preliminary breath tester (PBT). These are small-handheld units designed to give an officer a rough estimate of a person's level of alcohol content in their system. These are excellent to screen a person who has exhibited signs of impairment that may be due to things other than the large intake of alcohol, such as drugs or fatigue. Once arrested, however, a person is required to submit to a formal breath test, a blood test, or a urine test to determine the actual level of alcohol in their system. Which test is used is generally determined by local protocol, given the circumstances and the nature of the suspect's past history of impairment arrests. Repeat offenders are often given a blood test rather than breath, by rules established by the local prosecutor. Urine tests are very rare.

Blood tests are administered at a hospital or clinic by their trained staff at the request of the officer. The officer administers breath tests, or another officer will do so at a breath-testing site, often a local police department or public place. In the case of breath tests, the officers follow a step-by-step process, and the machine works through a series of both internal and external diagnostic tests.

Extensive protocol and the reliance on experts as to the validity of the results are part of the measures taken to ensure results are valid. Examples of protocol requirements include assurance by the officer that the subject about to give a breath test did not ingest anything for at least twenty minutes prior to a breath test. This includes assurance that the subject did not burp or vomit during this observational period. While a breath test is designed to test the deep-lung air from the subject, this observational period eliminates the contention that any residual intoxicant fluids where present in the mouth area that would influence the test result.

In all cases, officers must assure the subject had not ingested any additional alcohol from the time of arrest until the test was given, whether the test is by breath, blood, or urine. In addition, the breath test devices must run a successful internal test, where most also require testing a known alcohol sample at the same time. Officers should also assure the device is not in close proximity to outside influences, such as radio and cellular interference, although most modern devices incorporate internal sensors to prevent such interference.

Sometimes it is necessary to run a test twice. An error may have occurred in the first test, or impairment is obvious, but the breath test failed to show the presence of alcohol. Officers should investigate the source of the impairment further. This would be a strong indicator of drug impairment or a mental or medical condition. Prescription drugs, over-the-counter medicines, and illegal substances are becoming increasingly common products found in the blood of impaired drivers. While a breath test will not detect their presence, a blood or urine test will. Officers are also trained to look for medical signs that may appear to be impairment. The most common of these involve diabetics suffering from low blood sugar. In some rare cases, a brain injury or disease may contribute to observed symptoms of impairment.

The general level of prohibitive blood alcohol *per se* is .08 percent, but there are variations that indicate DUI, depending on things such as operation of a commercial motor vehicle and prior convictions, which may lower the prohibitive level, depending on a state's laws. The most important factor is the level of impairment. This is judged on the side of the road, well before any breath or blood test is given. This is the true measure of a person's danger to other drivers. How was their driving? What got the officer's attention to begin with? The blood or breath test only tells the officer what they already know—this person is impaired. The final results just serve to quantify the impairment.

When there are mixed or inconclusive results, and when appropriate, a blood test can be administered after a breath test. The blood can be screened later for the presence of any drugs that may be contributing to the observed impairment. Mixed or inconclusive results can come from the presence of drugs, either illegal or prescription, extreme fatigue, reduced mental capacity, or ingestion or expulsion of an intoxicant in close proximity to the time the test was given. Blood tests are best to eliminate these factors.

The test level may not rise to the *per se* level, but a conviction can still be possible, based on the pre-arrest observations of the officer. DUIs are not always determined with only objective information. The officer's observations, training, and experience can affect the next course of action. Each officer is different. Their experiences are different. Officers may rely on observations of others, witnesses, etc. The bottom line is that the person was arrested for impairment.

Legal Procedures

The paperwork completed during the course of a DUI investigation includes a citation, a notice of requirement to submit to the test, a series of follow-up questions, the test result forms, possible release forms, the officer narrative, and possibly a series of license suspension/revocation forms. The paperwork serves to track the entire case, provide guidance to the officers as to the details, and provide notice and information to the suspect. Both the prosecutor and the defense will use the reports to build their cases.

After individuals have been accused of DUI, they are given a court date and ordered to appear. Some may be incarcerated, pending a court appearance in the next few days. The timeline of court proceedings and officer involvement after the initial incident varies. Court dates can be the next day or several weeks away. Officers may not ever be needed if the case is settled. Otherwise, they may meet with the prosecutor prior to a preliminary hearing and motion hearing or an actual trial.

Some DUI cases are pled the next day. Others can go on for more than a year. Repeat offenders tend to extend much longer than first-time offenders. Repeat offenders face much more serious consequences and extended incarceration periods.

The most common misconceptions about the way officers handle DUI situations are that officers let most people go unless they are really bombed, and that officers are out there just to catch innocent people who are not really hurting anybody. Officers treat each case on its own merits and focus on protecting society from impaired drivers. Even if suspects are found not guilty, the officer stopped them from driving any farther that day. Who knows what might have happened otherwise?

When the case gets to court, the most common mistake made by DUI attorneys is assuming the officer is biased, or assuming the officer will not remember the case. The reason for these mistakes is usually that the case against their client is strong. The best way to punch holes in the case is to punch holes in the officers—as in the O.J. Simpson case.

Officers should approach these situations in a professional manner. They should be prepared to demonstrate their training and experience, but always remain professional. The arrest should have been conducted without bias, as part of the officer's duties. It should never be personal. It is incumbent upon each officer to be well-prepared to testify ahead of time. Reports should be reviewed, video and audiotapes gone over, and an adequate recall of the arrest event should be clear. Officers should testify as to what they recall and observed. If they do not recall, or don't know, they should say so, never speculating or guessing. The best education for DUI attorneys, to help them prepare for their cases and avoid such mistakes, is to ride along with officers making such arrests. They will observe the strengths and weaknesses of the process to best determine their approach to cases they will handle.

When testifying in court, the most important factors are honesty and being able to articulate the series of events that led the officer to make the arrest. Officers should review all the paperwork, review the videotape if one exists, and meet with the prosecutor ahead of time, if possible. The most important testimonies in court are what the officer observed and what it meant to him or her, as well as what the suspect said or did.

The most significant recent changes to drunken driving laws across America involve the reduction in the legal limit from .10 percent to .08 percent. Impairment is still obvious at .08 percent, and one's ability to safely operate a vehicle is compromised. This has resulted in most arrests and more convictions. As a result, some people have curtailed their alcohol intake to ensure they remain under the legal limit. Fewer impaired drivers equals less risk to others and safer roads for all users.

Officers may soon be using roadside evidentiary testing (probably breath). This could speed up the arrest process, putting officers back on the streets sooner. In addition, general acceptance of vehicle immobilization devices is growing. The most common of these are called ignition interlock devices that require the driver to blow into a test tube attached to the car's ignition before the car will start. Formerly ordered by courts to be placed on vehicles of multiple offenders, these devices are now being required by many states upon a person's first conviction for drunk driving. They appear to be having an impact by reducing a drunk driver's repeating behavior of drinking followed by driving.

Cases, Statutes, Regulations

Statutes relevant to the matters covered in this chapter include:

Operating under influence of intoxicant or other drug
    Wisc. Stat. 346.63 (1) (a) & (b):

Tests for intoxication; administrative suspension and court-ordered revocation
    Wisc. Stat. 343.305

Regulations relevant to this chapter can be found at the following site: http://www.dot.state.wi.us/safety/motorist/drunkdriving/law.htm

Major Dan Lonsdorf, the director of Wisconsin's Highway Safety Office, located in the Department of Transportation, is charged with coordinating highway safety behavioral improvement projects and programs. He is an executive board member of the Governor's Highway Safety Association.

As director, Major Lonsdorf oversees highway safety initiatives designed to improve the quality of life for all users of the state's transportation system. Besides supervising the Highway Safety Office, he is also director of State Patrol Commercial Vehicle Enforcement and Inspection Services and oversees the state's Chemical Breath Testing Section.

As a major in the highway patrol, Major Lonsdorf has broad experience in management of highway safety strategies, including supervising a vast range of state patrol traffic safety initiatives, such as aircraft and motorcycle patrols, work zone enforcement, crash reconstruction, and fleet management of more than 500 patrol cars. A state trooper for twenty-eight years, Major Lonsdorf patrolled the interstate highways around Wisconsin's capitol city of Madison, detecting and arresting more than 950 impaired drivers during his thirteen-year tenure as a patrol trooper.

From Traffic Stop to Prosecution

Faron W. Segotta

Chief

New Mexico State Police

ASPATORE

Testing and Interpretation

Driving is a multi-task function that is easily disrupted when alcohol is introduced into your body and ultimately your central nervous system; it impedes your ability to multi-task. When police officers initiate a traffic stop of a driver for suspected DWI, or driving while impaired, the officer is looking for some type of unusual driving behavior indicative of impairment, such as excessive speed or, conversely, a vehicle traveling well under the posted speed limit. Other indicators that police officers look for are drivers who stop short of a stop sign or a red light, drivers who are hesitant to react to the changing of a traffic signal, and drivers who fail to maintain a lane, weaving. These are some classic examples of driving behavior that alert a police officer that the driver may be impaired.

Beginning in 1975, the National Highway Traffic Safety Administration (NHTSA), sponsored research that led to the development of a DWI detection guide that listed twenty driving cues and the probabilities that a driver exhibiting a cue would have a BAC (blood alcohol content) of at least 0.10 percent (Harris et al., 1980; Harris, 1980). A similar study was conducted more recently that identified twenty-four driving cues that are predictive of DWI at the 0.08 level (Stuster, 1997); the latter study also identified ten post-stop cues with probabilities of DWI of at least 90 percent.

When a police officer has pulled over a suspected impaired driver, the officer will most likely ask the driver to exit the vehicle. This is important for a several reasons, as it will give the officer the ability to observe the driver's fine motor skills, such as balance and dexterity. Additionally, by having the driver exit the vehicle, the officer is attempting to minimize the risk of the driver fleeing. Once the driver is out of the vehicle, the officer will begin his or her observation of the driver. The officer will be looking for bloodshot or watery eyes, odor of alcohol on the breath of the driver, and any other sign of impairment. These clues and others are used by the officer to determine whether to go forward with his or her investigation by asking the driver to submit to a battery of field sobriety tests.

At the same time, NHTSA was providing officers with information concerning the driving behaviors that are the most predictive of impairment, the agency also sponsored research that led to the development of a standardized battery of tests for officers to administer to assess driver impairment after a traffic stop has been made. Marcelline Burns and Herbert Moskowitz conducted laboratory evaluations of several of the tests that were most frequently used by law enforcement officers at the time (Burns and Moskowitz, 1977).

Today most, if not all, law enforcement agencies use the NHSTA standardized field sobriety tests (SFSTs). The SFST battery is composed of three tests: Horizontal Gaze Nystagmus (HGN), Walk-and-Turn (WAT), and One-Leg Stand (OLS). NHTSA's SFSTs largely have replaced the invalidated performance tests of unknown merit that once were the patrol officer's only tools in helping make post-stop DWI arrest decisions. Additionally, the courts, prosecutors, and defense attorneys have become familiar with the SFSTs, which, for the most part, have been accepted as the standard for DWI investigations.

The SFSTs previously mentioned are:

The One-Leg Stand (OLS)

The officer will ask the driver to choose a leg to stand on and then instruct the driver to hold the opposite foot approximately six inches off the ground and while looking at their foot, count to thirty, all the while keeping their arms at their sides. When the driver has successfully completed the test, he or she may place the foot back on the ground. Prior to this test, the driver is asked if he or she has an injury or physical impairment that would affect the ability to perform the test. The clues the officer looks for are placing the foot on the ground before reaching thirty or using arms for balance, and miscounting.

The Walk-and-Turn (WAT)

The officer will find a flat, level surface utilizing a line, on the highway or sidewalk. The officer will instruct the driver to stand on the line with one foot in front of the other, heel-to-toe. When the driver has both feet on the line, he or she is instructed to step one foot in front of the other, heel-to-toe, for nine steps. When the driver has successfully completed the required nine steps, he or she should keep the back foot on the line, pivot on the line and turn full circle, and repeat the nine steps back, heel-to-toe, toward the officer. Again, the officer observes whether the driver can multi-task. The officer looks to see whether the driver steps heel-to-toe, whether he or she stays on the line, whether his or her arms are being raised for balance, and whether he or she can follow the instructions.

The Horizontal Gaze Nystagmus (HGN)

HGN is an involuntary jerking of the eye that occurs naturally as the eyes gaze to the side. Aschan (1958) described studies that linked various forms of nystagmus to BAC, and Wilkinson, Kime, and Purnell (1974) reported consistent changes in Horizontal Gaze Nystagmus with increasing doses of alcohol.

The officer begins by instructing the driver to stand with feet together, arms at the side. The officer places his finger twelve to eighteen inches from the driver's nose, and as the officer moves his finger from side to side, or approximately forty-five degrees from the center of the person's nose, the driver is instructed to follow the movement of the officer's finger without moving his or her head. Everyone has natural nystagmus, or jerking of the eye at approximately forty-five degrees from the center of the nose, referred to as maximum deviation. However, someone who is impaired will have involuntary jerking of the eye prior to forty-five degrees. Some of the clues the officer is looking for are whether the individual can follow the finger without moving his or her head; whether the involuntary jerking of the eye is present prior to forty-five degrees, or maximum deviation; and whether the person can follow directions. Alcohol affects the central nervous system, which affects one's ability to control involuntary muscle movements in the eye.

The HGN test is considered by many law enforcement officers to be the most effective technique to provide evidence of alcohol in a motorist's system. The normal variation in human physical and cognitive capabilities, and the effects of alcohol tolerance, can result in uncertainties when arrest decisions are made exclusively on the basis of physical and/or cognitive performance tests. These uncertainties have resulted in many DWI suspects being released rather than detained and transported to another location for evidentiary chemical testing. This is because some experienced drinkers can perform physical and cognitive tests acceptably, even with a BAC greater than 0.10 percent. However, experienced drinkers cannot conceal the physiological effects of alcohol from an officer who is skilled in HGN administration because Horizontal Gaze Nystagmus is an involuntary reaction over which an individual has absolutely no control.

Although the OLS, WAT, and HGN have been widely accepted as the SFSTs used by law enforcement to determine impairment, should someone have a physical impairment, such as a bad knee, leg, or back that may affect his or her ability to perform the OLS and WAT, the officer may ask the person to perform alternative tests to determine impairment. In some instances, drivers may be too impaired to perform the OLS and WAT because of increased risk of injury due to falling. However, every suspected impaired driver should be able to perform the HGN test.

Consequently, the officer can substitute other tests if he is unable to use one of the SFSTs. Another commonly used test is a simple finger-counting dexterity test. The driver is instructed to touch the pad of each finger with the pad of his thumb while counting out one, two, three, four, and then repeat the process in descending order. Again, the officer is looking for the driver's ability to multi-task. Some of the clues indicative of impairment are: Is the driver touching pad to pad? Does he or she start with the proper sequence, or do they miscount? Another alternative test is to ask the driver to recite the alphabet. The order does not matter when preparing for court, as long as you can demonstrate you gave the individual an opportunity to perform field sobriety tests.

The SFSTs described have certainly assisted law enforcement in the detection of drivers who are impaired from the effects of alcohol; however, the detection of drivers who are impaired because of the use of legal or illegal drugs has become a greater challenge for the law enforcement community. As a result, it has forced law enforcement agencies to train officers in this area. Officers who receive specialized training to detect drivers operating under the influence of drugs are known as drug recognition experts (DREs). A DRE is an individual who has successfully completed all phases of training requirements for certification established by the International Association of Chiefs of Police and the National Highway Traffic Safety Administration.

If the investigating officer believes that the defendant is impaired by a substance other than or in addition to alcohol, he may request that a DRE be called in to examine the defendant. The DRE then makes a determination as to whether the defendant is impaired, and if so, whether it is a result of a medical condition or drugs, and, if drugs, which of the seven drug categories is present. DREs learn to observe a suspect's appearance, behavior, performance of psychophysical tests, eyes in different lighting conditions, and vital signs to ascertain what category or categories of drugs have been used. A blood or urine sample is submitted to a laboratory for analysis and corroboration of the DRE's conclusion. Under "normal conditions," a person's pupils will react to changing lighting conditions— the pupils will dilate or constrict. The pupils of a person suspected to be under the influence of drugs will, in some instances, be unresponsive to changes in lighting conditions.

There is always a chance of inconclusive results with any battery of field sobriety tests. Therefore, when an officer has someone who shows all the signs of being impaired, yet when a breath sample is obtained and the defendant's breath alcohol content (BrAC) is below the legal limit or not consistent with the officer's filed observations based on the performance of the SFSTs by the driver, the officer should then determine if any factors could have influenced the BrAC, such as a delay in acquiring the BrAC sample. Sometimes in a remote area, it could be one-and-a-half or two hours before an officer arrives at a police station or booking facility. In those instances, the officer may want to subpoena an expert in the field of retrograde extrapolation. These experts are trained in the absorption and elimination of alcohol in the human body. Using retrograde extrapolation, an individual's approximate BrAC "range" can be determined at the time of arrest. It is a difficult process and usually reserved for the most serious of DWI cases—those that have resulted in a death or great bodily harm.

In addition, when the BrAC indicates a very small amount of alcohol or a reading of .00, or no alcohol, officers are trained to ask a series of questions of the driver to determine whether a preexisting medical condition could present symptoms similar to those of a person impaired by alcohol. These questions would allow the officer to determine whether there is something else affecting the driver's ability to operate a vehicle safely.

Although the administration of the SFSTs appears to be extensive and lengthy, a driver who pays attention and is not impaired can complete the SFSTs in less than fifteen minutes. If the driver is impaired and unable to follow instructions, then this process can take much longer to complete.

When it comes to recording the results of these tests, technology can play a significant role. Many agencies across the country that have specific DWI enforcement units require that all traffic stops of suspected impaired drivers be video- and audio-recorded. This trend is becoming more and more prevalent, particularly in New Mexico. However, because of this practice, defense attorneys use the recording of the stop and the performance of the SFSTs to refute the claims by law enforcement that their client performed poorly on the tests. It has been my experience that this defense is used in cases where the accused has performed marginally on the tests and is not obviously impaired. As they say, a picture paints a thousand words.

Upon completion of SFSTs and with sufficient evidence to believe the driver is impaired, he or she is placed under arrest and transported to a holding facility or police station, where the officer has access to a breathalyzer machine to test the breath alcohol content (BrAC). Every state has enacted a version of an implied consent law, which serves to encourage persons arrested for DWI to submit to a chemical test to determine blood alcohol content. Many states also allow for the testing of blood, breath, or urine for the presence of drugs. The concept of implied consent is that the state views the suspect as already having agreed to take the test, as a condition of operating a vehicle in the state. The typical wording of an implied consent law is as follows:

> Any person who operates a motor vehicle upon the public highways of this state shall be deemed to have given consent to a chemical test or tests for the purpose of determining the alcohol (or drug) content of his or her blood, when arrested for any act alleged to have been committed while the person was operating a vehicle while under the influence of alcohol (or any drug).

New Mexico's version of the Implied Consent Act can be found at [66-8-105 NMSA 1978].

Plainly stated, when you obtain your driver's license, you grant your permission to submit to a breath sample if you are arrested for an offense within the traffic code. Because of that, an individual who is arrested for DWI has given consent to this test. The Implied Consent warning is read to all suspects prior to the instructions on how to blow into the breathalyzer machine. The breathalyzer is a sophisticated piece of equipment that has the ability to capture a sample of a person's BrAC. Prior to administering the breath test, the breathalyzer performs an internal calibration to establish that it is working correctly. The suspect is then asked to provide a breath sample by blowing as hard and as long as possible into the mouthpiece of the breathalyzer. The breathalyzer automatically captures the breath sample at the precise moment. The breathalyzer provides a digital display of the suspect's BrAC, as well as a printed copy, if required.

Most states' breath-testing equipment is administered by the Department of Health or a state operated scientific laboratory. The accuracy of the instrument itself is rarely brought into question; however, the manner in which the officer administered the test and the required calibration checks of the testing equipment are frequently challenged by defense attorneys. As long as the officer can demonstrate that he or she is certified to operate the breathalyzer, administered the test pursuant to training, and complied with any other requirements of law pertaining to its use, challenges by the defense are easily quashed.

One common defense used in New Mexico courts is to challenge whether the officer observed the suspect for the standard twenty-minute deprivation period. The purpose of the deprivation period is to continuously observe the suspect for at least twenty minutes prior to obtaining a breath sample to ensure that the suspect did not introduce anything into his or her mouth that may affect the test results and to observe whether the suspect belched or vomited, as this may also affect the breath sample.

The presumptive level for impairment in most states is a BrAC reading of .08 percent, eight one-hundredths, or more. For example, New Mexico has a *per se* law of .08, so you are presumed driving while impaired if your BrAC is .08 or greater. NM ST § 66-8-110 (2008). Many states like New Mexico also have laws prohibiting a person from driving while under the influence of alcohol or drugs to a degree that renders him or her incapable of safely driving a vehicle. NM ST § 66-8-102 (2008).. Although a BrAC of .08 or greater is ideal, it does not preclude an officer from charging a suspected impaired driver with DWI if his or her BrAC is less than the presumptive level, .08. A BrAC below the presumptive level means the officer will have to strengthen his or her case through other evidence. Often a police officer will obtain a blood sample from suspected impaired drivers whose BrAC is below .08. A blood sample is one of the most reliable methods of determining the alcohol concentration level of a person and is not easily refuted.

The process of documenting the enforcement stop will serve a very important function in the successful prosecution of a suspected impaired driver. The necessary reports will document the officer's interaction with the individual from the observation of erratic driving, the initial contact with the driver, the performance of the SFSTs, and the administration of the breath test. All of these things will be indicative of a successful prosecution. In fact, much of this documentation will be required by the courts. Therefore, an officer will want to demonstrate his or her probable cause for the stop by issuing a traffic citation for the violation of the law observed.

For example, if a driver failed to maintain a lane, this violation becomes the officer's probable cause to initiate the traffic stop. Some jurisdictions require a probable cause statement, indicating the facts as observed by the arresting officer. The arresting officer will most likely issue a citation specifically for DWI. In most states, that is required. Another requirement may be an affidavit for arrest of the accused. These documents vary from state to state, but are necessary as the officer builds a case based upon articulable facts, basically the things that an officer can use as testimony in court.

Legal Aspects

In preparation for trial, a police officer may attend a pre-trial conference with the prosecuting attorney to review the case to see whether there are any issues the defense may raise. The timeline for a pre-trial conference depends on the number of DWI cases pending prosecution and the caseload of the court. In New Mexico and other states, DWI cases have to be brought before the court within six months of the arrest. Continuances are allowed and commonly approved, but in most cases, the court likes to have the case wrapped up from the date of arrest to the date of prosecution in no more than six months.

Usually it is the caseload of the court that will determine the length of this process. For instance, in a metropolitan area handling thousands of cases a year, the actual adjudication of the case is commonly protracted. Sometimes other factors inhibit the prosecution of a case, such as waiting for analysis of a blood or urine sample from the testing laboratory.

Probably the most common thing defense attorneys look for relates to the manner in which the SFSTs were conducted—particularly whether the arresting officer gave the proper instructions on the SFSTs and observed all the clues that are indicative of a person who may be impaired.

The validity of SFST results depends on police officers following the established, standardized procedures for test administration and scoring. NHTSA's *SFST Student Manual* states that the procedures demonstrated in the training program describe how SFSTs should be administered under ideal conditions, but that ideal conditions do not always exist in the field. Variations from ideal conditions and deviations from the standardized procedures might affect the evidentiary weight that should be given to test results.

Courts in several states have reviewed the admissibility of field sobriety tests that assess physical coordination and have held that deviations in the administration of the tests should not result in the suppression of test results. These courts have found that field sobriety tests, including the Walk-and-Turn and the One-Leg-Stand of the SFST battery, are simple physical dexterity exercises that can be interpreted by an officer in the field and by others in a court of law.

The HGN test has become an issue recently. The courts have ruled that the admissibility of the HGN test may be treated differently because of its "scientific nature." For this reason, HGN results are vulnerable to challenge and likely to be excluded by the court if the test was not administered in strict compliance with established protocols. Other states have been even less accommodating to deviations from the standardized procedures.

In particular, the Ohio State Supreme Court ruled that law enforcement officers have no discretion in the administration of SFSTs. In a four-to-two decision, the Ohio State Supreme Court held in *Ohio v. Homan,* 732 N.E.2d 952 (Ohio 2000), that Standardized Field Sobriety Tests conducted in a manner that departs from the methods established by NHTSA "are inherently unreliable" and thus inadmissible.

It is the opinion of the writer that the case load for prosecuting attorneys is such that the most common mistake in DWI prosecution is the mere fact that the prosecuting attorney does not spend a lot of time getting to know the case. In some of these instances, if there is a pre-trial conference, it occurs on the day of the trial as the attorney is trying to prepare for multiple cases. Sad to say, DWI in some areas of the country has not reached the level of importance that it requires. Approximately 15,000 deaths occur each year because of drinking and driving, and that is alarming. Unfortunately, new prosecutors begin their careers prosecuting low-level cases, which are usually DWI, without having the benefit of appropriate training. I would encourage attorneys handling DWI cases to partner with local law enforcement and observe DWI detection and apprehension techniques to include the administration of SFSTs. The experience gained in the field better prepares an attorney to successfully prosecute these cases.

When a case is set for trial, every officer involved in the case will be subpoenaed to testify. During the trial, an officer will have to establish several facts—for example, that he or she was on duty, in uniform, and displaying the badge of office at the time of the enforcement stop. The officer has to establish venue and that he or she had jurisdiction. The officer will have to articulate the probable cause for the stop and then describe in detail the entire traffic stop. If the stop was captured on video, the officer may point out specific things to the judge and jury.

Preparation for trial is essential and requires the officer to review the case prior to trial. To prepare officers for trial, many agencies put officers through mock trials during their training. The officer will review his or her case file with the prosecuting attorney, examining the strengths, as well as the weaknesses, of each case.

Most police officers are required to attend some form of specialized law enforcement training at a law enforcement academy or prescribed training facility. During that initial training, the officer will receive instruction on topics specific to DWI. Additionally, officers may receive refresher training throughout their careers. In New Mexico, the state legislature has taken interest in the types of training mandated for continued certification of all New Mexico police officers. Every two years, New Mexico police officers must complete forty hours of training, some of which is mandated by the state legislature. Recently SFSTs have been added to the training curriculum to better prepare New Mexico police officers to remove impaired drivers from New Mexico highways and to help prepare the officers for successful prosecution of DWI cases.

The manner in which DWI cases are handled by law enforcement depends on where DWI enforcement efforts are placed in terms of priority in the agency. If DWI initiatives are not made a priority by the chief of police or the governing body, then they do not become a priority for the patrol officers who are out in the field enforcing DWI laws. This is where law enforcement needs to do a better job making DWI a priority. No state in the nation is immune from death and destruction caused by impaired drivers. If the governing body or law enforcement leaders will not make DWI a priority and dedicate proactive policing measures to target drunk drivers, then those agencies will not experience the success that other agencies have demonstrated.

DWI detection and apprehension is not sought after, unfortunately, by every police officer in the field for a variety of reasons. People who are impaired are not cooperative, so they occupy a considerable amount of the officer's time following an arrest for DWI. The time required to process a single DWI arrest can be as much as four hours, depending on your jurisdiction.

Additionally, officers would rather spend time in the field than testifying in court. The experience of testifying in court can be uncomfortable for officers, particularly those who do not routinely arrest impaired drivers. It is common for defense attorneys to gather information on an officer's work history regarding DWI arrests by asking the officer how many suspected drunk drivers he or she has arrested in the past. If an officer is arresting only one or two impaired drivers every three months or so, his or her skill set will not be as sharp as that of an officer who is arresting two or three impaired drivers a week. This could present a potential problem, as the arresting officer may not follow all the procedures while administering the SFSTs, obtaining the breath sample, or any other requirements prescribed by law, because he or she just does not do it as frequently as others.

Educating prosecuting attorneys in all the aspects of DWI detection and apprehension is crucial. When you brief the case or prepare for the trial, if the attorney prosecuting the case has received the same training as the police officer and observed the officer in the field, preparing for trial is much easier. When an officer discusses items such as the clues observed while conducting the field sobriety test, the prosecuting attorney can immediately relate. This gives the attorney a better foundation from which to ask questions of the officer. If an attorney knows what the officer needs to say, the attorney can prompt the officer with the correct questions without leading the officer.

For example the attorney may say, "Tell us about the clues you saw during the field sobriety tests." This will prompt the officer to be thorough and descriptive when describing the SFSTs. Talking with an attorney while preparing for any case is very simple, but the minute you get up on the witness stand and take the oath, things change. You need to know your case well and be able to articulate the facts of the case in a clear and concise manner. Prosecuting attorneys must keep the officer focused and on point, redirect the officer back on target, and help him or her through that process. The judge and jury will be listening closely to the testimony and reviewing it to determine the guilt or innocence of the accused.

DWI is no longer socially acceptable; penalties in many states have increased dramatically over the years. Subsequently, those arrested for DWI obtain an attorney, making it imperative that law enforcement utilize best practices when encountering impaired drivers. Twenty-five years ago, when I began my law enforcement career, you rarely saw a person charged with

DWI retain an attorney; however, today, with increased penalties, it is rare that the accused is not represented by counsel.

Law enforcement has made tremendous progress regarding DWI, and there is still much work to be done. We must continue to sharpen our skills and actively pursue every impaired driver to ensure the safest highways possible for all.

In October 1982, Chief Faron W. Segotta was commissioned a New Mexico State Police officer and has served in various assignments throughout New Mexico. Chief Segotta has held the ranks of patrol officer, sergeant, lieutenant, captain, major, deputy chief and adjutant chief. On March 8, 2006, he was appointed by Governor Richardson as the nineteenth chief of the New Mexico State Police. Chief Segotta also serves as the deputy cabinet secretary of the Department of Public Safety.

Chief Segotta oversees 800 commissioned police officers and 300 civilian support personnel. He has more than twenty-five years of service with the department in a vast array of assignments.

A 1993 graduate of Northwestern University School of Police Staff and Command, a 2001 graduate of the FBI Southwest Command College, and a graduate of the FBI National Executive Institute Session #30, Chief Segotta holds an Executive Level Law Enforcement Certification, awarded by the New Mexico Law Enforcement Academy. He is a member of the International Association of Chiefs of Police, president of the New Mexico Chiefs of Police Association, executive board member of the New Mexico Law Enforcement Academy, and an executive board member of SAFER New Mexico Now.

Chief Segotta brings a forward-thinking approach to law enforcement that utilizes a collaboration of federal, state, county, and community resources to address public safety concerns in New Mexico.

Dedication: *I would like to dedicate this chapter to my wife, Mickie, and my children, Benjamin, Faira, and Zachary, for allowing me to pursue my career. You have sacrificed many things along the way, and for that, I am forever grateful.*

Detecting, Arresting, and Processing the Impaired Driver

Michael L. Asleson

Major

Minnesota State Patrol

ASPATORE

Initial Observations: Determining Whether Someone Is Driving While Impaired

Determining and proving that someone is legally impaired is a lengthy, complex, and critically important task. Impairment can be caused by many things, including alcohol, legal and illegal drugs, fatigue, and a variety of other distractions. The focus of this chapter explores issues related to driving while impaired (DWI) due to alcohol consumption.

The vast majority of DWI arrests in Minnesota are made after an LEO (law enforcement officer) has made contact with an impaired driver following a traffic stop or the driver's involvement in a traffic crash. Minnesota DWI law prohibits driving, operating, or being in physical control of a motor vehicle while under the influence of alcohol, so there are a few times when drivers are arrested for DWI because they are impaired while having the present ability to drive. A common example of a physical control DWI arrest would be an intoxicated person sleeping behind the wheel of his or her vehicle on the side of the road with the keys for the vehicle in their possession, but the vehicle not actually running. (See Appendix A for the Minnesota State Highway Patrol DWI Policy.)

When an officer stops an impaired driver, the officer may have a significant initial suspicion of impairment based on the driving behavior observed, or the officer may have no suspicion of impairment whatsoever. Many impaired drivers are arrested for DWI after they have been stopped for a traffic, equipment, or registration violation that gives the officer no hint that the driver may be impaired. It is often during the face-to-face discussion between driver and officer that the officer first detects signs or clues of impairment.

The most common observations of the driver in these cases are the combination of the odor of an alcoholic beverage on the breath, eyes that are bloodshot and/or glassy, speech that is slurred, and a flushed face. Other suspicious signs include inconsistent or illogical answers to questions, evasive behaviors, demonstrated difficulty dividing his or her attention, or problems performing otherwise simple tasks, such as obtaining documents from the glove box or getting identification from his or her wallet.

There are other times when an officer is highly suspicious of impairment early as a direct result of driving conduct. NHTSA (National Highway Traffic and Safety Administration) has developed a list of twenty driving behaviors that have been linked to impaired driving. The data resulted from a comprehensive review of DWI arrest reports and the driving clues that drew the arresting officers' attention in those arrests. Research of the reports allowed NHTSA to attach a percentage reliability factor to each of the driving behaviors. Examples of the twenty driving behaviors are:

1. Turning with a wide radius
2. Straddling center of lane marker
3. Appearing to be drunk (based on posture, gestures, etc.)
4. Almost striking object or vehicle
5. Weaving
6. Driving on other than designated highway
7. Swerving
8. Speed more than ten miles per hour below limit
9. Stopping without cause in traffic lane
10. Following too closely
11. Drifting
12. Tires on center or lane marker
13. Braking erratically
14. Driving into opposing or crossing traffic
15. Signaling inconsistent with driving actions
16. Slow response to traffic signals
17. Stopping inappropriately (other than in lane)
18. Turning abruptly or illegally
19. Accelerating or decelerating rapidly
20. Driving with headlights off

In my experience, one of the best indicators of impaired driving is a weaving vehicle. This weaving can be extremely subtle and even contained within the lane. A traffic lane of twelve or even ten feet allows for significant lateral drift of a vehicle without departure from the lane. The trained officer is watchful for a repeated weaving pattern, as the weaving action often is the result of the impaired driver's inability to perform the otherwise relatively simple task of driving the vehicle in a straight line. Often the weaving is more aggressive, and the vehicle departs from its lane of travel; this action is quickly followed by the driver's realization that the vehicle is out of its lane, which he or she then attempts to correct by abruptly placing the vehicle back into the lane of travel. When this action is repeated several times, it helps rule out that the possibility that the driver departed from the lane as the result of a momentary distraction or some other reason not related to impairment.

Other strong indicators of impaired driving include fluctuations in speed for no apparent reason and a failure to dim headlights before oncoming vehicles on two-lane roadways. Other impaired drivers may indicate their condition by making wide turns or responding slowly or not at all to traffic signals. Of course, the more individual errors displayed by a driver, the greater the probability that the driver is in fact impaired by alcohol, drugs, fatigue, or distraction.

After the Crash: Assessing the Driver's Impairment

When an impaired driver is involved in a traffic crash, there are a variety of possible circumstances, and thus, a number of different ways in which the officer will contact the driver. The driver may be sitting or even pinned behind the steering wheel. Such circumstances make the determination of who was driving an easy one, but often the officer will face situations in which the driver may have fled from the scene or intentionally blended in with passengers and bystanders. Often no one admits to being the driver; sadly, I have heard the cold, "I wasn't driving" response by impaired drivers even after they have been responsible for the death of their passenger friends.

Usually it is during the face-to-face discussion between the officer and the driver or suspected driver that the officer gains the various indicators of impairment. There may be additional information that raises the officer's suspicion, such as reports of the involved vehicle being driven erratically prior to the crash, or visible alcohol containers in and around the crashed vehicle. When determining the driver's level of sobriety, the officer has the responsibility to take into consideration that the driver may be injured because of the crash and needs to ascertain that indicators of impairment such as staggering and slurred speech are not the result of a medical injury.

As with a traffic stop, the officer must be alert to the odor of an alcoholic beverage on the driver's breath, as well as cover-up odors, such as mints or gum, which the driver may be using to mask evidence of alcohol consumption. If the driver is outside of the vehicle, the officer should be alert to the mental and physical abilities of the driver. The officer must be attentive to how the driver speaks and divides his or her attention and to the condition of his or her eyes. If the driver is not physically injured, the officer can ask the driver to perform a full battery of field sobriety tests at the scene of the crash.

If a driver is seriously injured or unconscious, the officer may have very limited observation opportunities with respect to the driver's physical condition. It is possible that the officer's only suspicion of impairment has come from observations of witnesses and the paramedics who treated the driver. Other indicators include the presence of alcohol containers and an odor of alcoholic beverage on the driver's breath.

Unlike other controlled substances that also cause impairment, alcohol tends to affect most people the same way. With alcohol DWI stops, I am always alert to the odor of an alcoholic beverage on drivers' breath, whether their speech is slurred, whether their eyes are bloodshot and glassy, how they respond to questions, and their general physical dexterity.

During the standardized field sobriety testing (SFST) battery, described below, we measure the driver's ability to divide his or her attention—that is, doing something physical and something mental at the same time. Divided attention tests are not given to trick the driver. They are given to help an officer determine whether the driver is impaired. Driving is itself a divided-attention task. A driver performs multiple physical and mental tasks simultaneously, and alcohol affects one's ability to divide attention between the two. An impaired driver can often perform a single task without difficulty. They can answer a question or obtain a document from their wallet. However, alcohol impairs their ability to perform physical and mental tasks simultaneously. Therefore, the SFST battery fairly and accurately tests the driver's physical and mental abilities.

One key piece of information that an officer must remember when interviewing a suspected impaired driver is that the first thing alcohol affects is one's judgment. Therefore, an officer should be alert to the driver making bad or irrational decisions that could harm the officer. Impairment may cause an otherwise respectful and reasonable citizen to drive away from the officer, or it may cause an otherwise passive person to become aggressive and to confront the officer physically. The officer must also be alert to the actions of passengers in the vehicle, as well as passing traffic. Officers are too frequently struck at roadside during traffic stops, many of them DWI arrests; in fact, more officers are killed today in traffic crashes than by felonious assault. Also, intoxicated passengers, lacking the judgment they would otherwise have, sometimes come to the aid of their driver friend, and the "group think" phenomenon can lead to poor judgment and pose a serious threat to the solo arresting officer.

The Process of Administering Field Sobriety Tests

Many law enforcement agencies have policies guiding officers on which field sobriety tests should be used. There are three that are the most common around the country and that have been scientifically validated through NHTSA research. They are referred to as the Standardized Field Sobriety Tests (SFSTs). These tests are extremely effective in helping officers determine whether a driver is impaired and whether he or she is above or below the legal limit. There is a great deal of information and background available about these tests, the research behind them, the training manuals, etc., through sources such as NHTSA's Web site: http://www.nhtsa.dot.gov/people/injury/alcohol/SFST/introduction.htm.

One of the most reliable tests, and in my opinion the best of all the screenings, is the Horizontal Gaze Nystagmus test, or HGN. Nystagmus is a fancy word that means the involuntary jerking of the eye. One of the best things about the HGN test is that the driver is powerless to manipulate his or her performance. To do so would be like trying to change one's own blood pressure. It is also an excellent test because people's various tolerances to alcohol do not change their responses to the test: It is not a test one can "improve" at or practice for. It is also quick and non-intrusive.

To perform the HGN test, the officer simply holds an object, such as a finger, pen light, or pen, in front of the driver's eyes. After the officer has ruled out neurological problems by verifying that the eyes can track equally and that pupil size is relatively similar, the test begins. The first part of the test is to view whether each eye tracks smoothly as the eyes move relatively quickly from side to side. A commonly used analogy is whether the eye tracks from side to side like a marble over a piece of polished glass (as a sober person's eye does) or whether it makes jerky movements, like the same marble over a piece of coarse sandpaper. The second clue is to cause the eye track to maximum deviation and observe whether there is distinct jerking—or nystagmus—when the eye is held for at least four seconds in that position. The last portion of the test determines whether there is the onset of nystagmus prior to forty-five degrees; that is, whether *any* nystagmus begins before the eye reaches a forty-five-degree angle from center. Officers spend significant time in a two- or three-day SFST training course to learn how to properly administer these tests and interpret their results.

The second test in the SFST battery is the Walk-and-Turn (WAT) test. In this test, drivers are asked to stand in a heel-to-toe position, right foot directly in front of the left, with arms down at the sides. They are asked to remain in that position while the rest of the test is explained; they are then asked to confirm that they understand the test thus far. The officer then instructs the driver to walk nine steps in a heel-to-toe fashion. The officer provides a partial demonstration, instructing and demonstrating to the driver how to walk heel-to-toe and how to turn at the end of the first nine steps. This is followed by the instruction to walk nine heel-to-toe steps back to where the driver started. The instructions to the driver include that they are to watch their feet during the test, count their steps aloud, and keep their arms down at their sides. They are also instructed not to stop the test after they have begun. Again, drivers are asked to confirm whether they understand the instructions, after which they are told to begin. As described earlier, this test intentionally divides the suspect's attention, requiring them to do something physical and something mental simultaneously.

During the WAT test, the officer looks for a number of clues. During the instruction stage, the officer watches for whether the driver starts too soon and whether he or she is unable to maintain balance during the instructions. During the test, the officer will watch for whether the driver sways while walking, steps off the line, stops during the test, does not touch heel-to-toe, makes an incorrect turn, or takes an incorrect number of steps.

The last SFST is the One-Leg Stand (OLS). In this test, drivers are asked to stand with their feet side-by-side and arms kept down at their sides during the instructions. The driver is then instructed to lift one of his or her feet, keeping the foot about six inches off the ground with the toe pointed forward. Both legs are to be kept straight, and the driver is to look at the elevated foot while he or she counts aloud: "one thousand one, one thousand two," and so on until told to stop. The officer monitors the time, and the test lasts thirty seconds. The officer watches for whether the driver sways during the test, uses his or her arms to balance, puts the foot down, hops, or is unable to perform the test at all.

Other tests are helpful and often used, even though they do not have the scientifically validated research attached to them. One of these involves simply having the person recite the alphabet—a simple test for a sober person, but at times difficult for someone who is impaired. Another is to count backwards from identified numbers, such as from seventy-nine to fifty-four. There is also a screening known as the Romberg test, which involves a set of instructions that includes having a driver touch the tip of his or her nose with an index finger. There are also relatively non-intrusive tests, such as having the driver touch his or her thumb to each of the fingers on that hand and back again. All of these tests are helpful to the officer in making the ultimate decision of whether the driver is impaired.

At the conclusion of these tests, generally the driver is asked to submit to a PBT (preliminary/portable breath testing device). The admissibility of these tests varies from state to state. In Minnesota, the PBT is a pre-arrest test with limited admissibility in court; however, these devices have evolved through the years and are amazingly reliable. The model we use is made by Intoximeter and is known as the Alco-Sensor IV. It is my understanding that about a dozen states use this type of device for their post-arrest evidentiary test, giving credence to the reliability and accuracy of today's pre-arrest field testing devices.

Interpreting the Test Results

The result of the PBT test provides the officer with some important pieces of information. First, it affirms the suspicion that the impairment the officer already noted is (or is not) due to alcohol. If there is noticeable impairment and no presence of alcohol, obviously the officer must alter his or her investigation to a DWI-controlled substance interview that may involve a DRE (drug recognition expert). Second, it provides greater insight as to the level of the driver's alcohol concentration. It is the policy of our agency to inform the driver of the PBT test result upon request of the driver or his or her attorney. That may not be the case with different agencies.

While the PBT result is not admissible in the criminal trial, it is an important test, and one that is admissible in the civil processes resulting from the arrest. The civil processes vary, depending on the circumstances of the arrest and the driver's record of past DWI arrests. In our state, the civil sanctions progressively include the revocation of the driver's license, the impoundment of license plates, and, in some cases, the seizure of the motor vehicle.

The SFSTs take only a few minutes to perform. Even if an officer conducts HGN, the Walk-and-Turn, One-Leg Stand, and other miscellaneous tests, as well as a PBT, the total time required to complete the process is less than ten minutes. Because an evidentiary post-arrest test might not be obtained or may be deemed inadmissible, officers should conduct the SFSTs whenever safely possible and record their multiple observations as thoroughly as possible.

The procedure then is for the officer to record the observations from these tests onto a DWI report. In our case, the information is recorded on sheets contained in a uniform DWI packet. Some of the information is also contained electronically into the CAD (computer aided dispatching) log itself. After the arrest, these observations are incorporated into a narrative arrest report. (See Appendix B for a sample DWI Arrest Report.)

When reaching a determination about the driver's impairment, the trained officer should take into consideration *all* of the evidence available about this person before making the arrest decision. The drivers' actions behind the wheel, the results of their SFSTs, their perceived ability to process information, and their physical ability to balance and perform simple functions should all be taken into consideration. Except for the unconscious or injured driver in a crash, there are often multitudes of things the officer adds up to determine whether the driver is impaired.

If the SFSTs are considered independently (which they are actually not in practice), the HGN has six clues. An officer's decision point for that test alone is that if four or more clues exist, the officer can be confident that the driver has over .08 percent blood alcohol content. In the walk and turn test, the decision point is two clues out of several. The one leg stand also has a decision point on its own of two clues. However, combining the results of the HGN and WAT—or all three tests—significantly increases the validity of the test results. As illustrated in the table below, which is taken from a NHTSA Web site, combined test results can achieve an accuracy of 91 percent, which is an impressive level of certainty. Again, it is on the totality of the evidence and observations that an arrest is made, and not on a single observation or test.

Table 1 Comparison of SFST Accuracy During the 1981 and 1998 Validation Studies		
SFST(s)	**% Correct Decisions 1981**	**% Correct Decisions 1998**
SFST(s) 1981 1998 SFST Battery (the 3 tests combined)	81	91
Horizontal Gaze Nystagmus (HGN)	77	88
Walk-and-Turn (WAT)	68	79
One-Leg Stand (OLS)	65	83

This table is taken from one of many sites that offer further and more detailed information about the SFSTs:
http://www.nhtsa.dot.gov/portal/site/nhtsa/menuitem.18e416bf1b09b6b bbf30811060008a0c/

An officer doesn't look at the results of any single test in isolation. The officer needs to consider everything that has been gained through his or her senses. The officer should consider the driving conduct, the driver's physical appearance, the condition of their eyes, how the driver spoke, their ability to divide their attention, and the results of the various SFSTs, including the PBT, if provided, before making the decision of whether to arrest or release the driver.

Scientific Tests that Are Performed

Once an arrest is made, an officer has three evidentiary tests from which to choose, although states differ in terms of what the officer must provide. In Minnesota, the officer may offer just the breath test as an option. The driver has the choice of taking a breath test or refusing. In our state, the criminal and civil consequences for refusing are significant. Even without a prior alcohol-related driving offense, a driver's refusal to test in the state of Minnesota can result in a one-year driver's license revocation. Further, the driver is charged with the original DWI offense in addition to the separate gross misdemeanor offense of refusing to submit to testing. A gross misdemeanor carries a maximum penalty of up to one year in jail and fine of up to $3,000. *See Also* https://www.revisor.leg.state.mn.us/ and https://www.revisor.leg.state.mn.us/bin/getpub.php?type=s&num=169A.26 &year=2006.

The breath test is completed on an Intoxilyzer 5000; it is a common practice in our state for the arresting officer to run the test because of the relatively automated and tamper-proof design of this device.

If an Intoxilyzer is unavailable, or if there are other reasons breathe testing is not an option (e.g., a limiting physical condition of the driver or an injured driver who must stay in the hospital), then the officer may choose to offer blood or urine as the test option. In Minnesota, the officer may offer one or the other, but it is not possible to document an actual refusal unless an alternative test is offered and refused, as well. In essence, the driver would have the choice of taking a urine or blood test when a breath test is not offered.

The officer will consider a number of factors in determining which test to pursue. As stated above, the availability of an Intoxilyzer will strongly dictate whether a breath test is offered. The physical condition of a driver will also be a factor. It would not be prudent to waste time having someone who is physically impaired attempt to provide an adequate breath sample. Other factors that must be considered are how busy a testing facility is at the time and whether the breath testing room is backed up. The goal is for the officer to secure a test that will be admissible and that allows him or her to return to patrol duties as soon as possible.

Breath testing devices (Intoxilyzers) are located throughout the state, generally inside the law enforcement center. We also have a couple of mobile units inside large testing vehicles for special field purposes.

The blood test is generally taken at a hospital but can also be taken by an authorized medical person at a jail facility or other location if necessary or prudent. The urine test can be obtained virtually anywhere, as long as the required privacy is provided.

The most reliable piece of evidence in a DWI case, in my opinion, is the evidentiary alcohol-concentration result. Whereas all other observations are arguably subjective, even with scientific validity behind them, the scientific test result treats everyone the same. If a driver is over the per se limit (.08), then he or she is prohibited from driving.

Other issues certainly come into play when determining which scientific tests should be administered; these include how bad the driving was and the condition of the driver's physical and mental ability. After the arrest, other factors must be considered, as well, including the driver's past driving record, how high his or her test result was, and whether the driver had other passengers, particularly children, in the car. All of these elements will affect the severity of the particular DWI arrest. (See Appendix C for Minnesota's Motor Vehicle Implied Consent Advisory and Appendix D for the state's Implied Consent Law Peace Officer's Certificate.)

Dealing with Mixed or Inconclusive Results

As stated earlier, a complete array of factors must be considered before an officer makes an arrest/no arrest decision. In this way, the process can be equated to treating an injury; symptoms are similar from patient to patient, but each person is unique and might react differently.

For example, an officer may be faced with a driver who displays the maximum number of clues on HGN and has an extremely high alcohol-concentration (AC) on the PBT, yet performs the WAT and OLS flawlessly. This may be because the driver has a high tolerance to alcohol due to frequent or even excessive use. On the other hand, police may encounter someone who displays minimal clues during the HGN test and actually tests below the legal limit on the PBT but can hardly walk. This might be due to relatively low experience with alcohol or the involvement of other substances. Such test results may even indicate that the driver is heavily fatigued. Over my thirty-one-year career, one of the most intoxicated drivers I have ever stopped was a young male driving on Interstate 94 in Minneapolis. He had been drinking in Wisconsin and was returning home. He took up three freeway lanes and both shoulders as I followed him. That's a lateral distance of fifty-six feet, and the weaving was continuous from shoulder curb to median barrier wall. He then vomited in the back seat of my squad—yet he tested only .08. Comparatively, an experienced drinker may not even feel affected at .08 or may display only minimal clues of note to the officer.

Regardless of the situation, the guiding principle is for officers to be as complete as possible with all of the testing and to record everything completely their reports. It is of paramount importance to avoid leaving anything out of the testing itself or the recording of that information.

The arresting officer is responsible for providing as much information to others downstream in the criminal justice system about the driver and the observations and the testing that lead to the arrest. The admissibility of evidentiary tests must be safeguarded to the degree possible by the arresting officer by taking concrete measures to ensure that results are accurate. In our state, blood and urine tests are analyzed in the laboratory of the BCA (Bureau of Criminal Apprehension). Chemists are called on at times to describe their testing procedures and safeguards in court, and in my experience, they are knowledgeable and credible witnesses.

In the case of a breath test on the Intoxilyzer, in our state we take two separate breath samples, and each sample is analyzed twice by the instrument and an automated testing sequence. Consequently, we actually end up with four test results from two separate breath tests, which are then compared to each other. The Intoxilyzer testing process also requires the testing of a known alcohol-concentration often referred to as the simulator solution. Between the two subject tests, the instrument tests the simulator solution, and we must ensure that the instrument analyzes that known AC correctly. All of the records are electronically collected and printed in an official report. The driver receives a copy of that printed report.

Handling Borderline Results

One challenging "borderline" situation for the officer is when he or she is dealing with a driver who is slightly impaired and, pre-arrest, measures right at or slightly above the legal limit. The officer knows that if he or she arrests the driver, the driver will be lower than the legal limit by the time an evidentiary test is taken. If a great deal of bad driving or visible physical impairment was not observed, the DWI arrest will likely be reduced. The officer rightfully questions whether the involved arrest process is worth what the end outcome will be. Yet the officer is concerned about liability: What if he or she releases the driver and a crash occurs down the road?

While I do not necessarily support this response, there are times in those cases where the officer will offer the driver an arrangement at the scene: an example would be having a more sober person drive from that location. If the driver is alone, sometimes officers will offer a tow truck to take his or her vehicle. Having someone else drive is not a difficult arrangement, but having a vehicle towed or parked is more complicated, given the lack of a legal basis for any compelled towing of the vehicle.

The Timeline of Events after a DUI Accusation

Once the officer has completed the DWI arrest process, there is the completion and submission of reports. Paperwork is probably one of the greatest reasons that some officers opt to not arrest impaired drivers or avoid it to the degree possible. It has been said that a DWI arrest involves more paperwork than a house closing. We have a DWI arrest packet that includes some of the basic forms. The DWI arrest report is two pages that require the basic information about the driver, vehicle, time, and location, as well as officer observations about driving and impairment (Appendix A). The officer completes this portion of the arrest report during the actual arrest to avoid forgetting details at a later date. Some of this information is also contained in a narrative arrest report completed shortly after the arrest, such as the end of shift or the following day.

Anything the officer observes, smells, or hears during the interview with the driver should be contained in the report. The most effective DWI enforcement officers are those whose reports contain everything they have observed, leaving out no details, regardless of how unimportant they may seem at the time. The more observations the officer records about the driver, the less effective a defense attorney can be at dismissing the observation or attributing it to some other cause. Surely, any driver who is stopped will be nervous, and as a result, some of the officer's observations of a driver could be attributed to nerves. Additionally, it is important to remember that a driver may have the odor of an alcoholic beverage on his or her breath, but not be driving illegally. However, officers who have fully observed and recorded all of the things their senses have picked up will be more effective during the criminal justice process in convincing others that their allegation that the driver was impaired is in fact fair and valid.

Further, test results are sometimes not available for trial. They might be lost or ruled inadmissible for a variety of reasons. Therefore, the officer with the most complete observations who details them into a well-prepared arrest report is well able to handle this situation, as he or she will not be overly reliant on an evidentiary test that might not be available for reasons beyond their control.

A number of people depend on complete and accurate arrest report packets. These people include the prosecutor, judge, probation officer, the officer's agency and supervisor, the defense attorney, driver and vehicle services (for actions against driver's license, license plates, and vehicle), and other individuals and agencies. The packet provides them with insight to and documentation of the arrest. In addition, and perhaps most importantly to the officer, it will remind the officer of his or her observations, decisions, and actions at a much later date. There is virtually no way for an active DWI officer to remember the multiple observations and clues contained in one arrest report months later, when the arrest and not-guilty plea find their way into a courtroom. The arrest report is essential for that required recall and memory refreshment.

Once the paperwork is complete, that is often the last time the officer has dealings with the arrested or involved driver. A certain percentage of the cases will resurface as accused drivers request court or jury trials, or use civil hearings to contest the action taken against their driver's licenses, license plates, or vehicles. If force was used during the arrest and/or a complaint was filed against the officer for some type of alleged misconduct, the arrest may be relived during an interview review process, such as an internal affairs investigation.

Some of our courts are working hard to "fast track" the DWI arrest so that the trial is held within a couple months of the arrest. Sadly, however, there are times when a trial resulting from a DWI arrest takes place a year or more after the arrest.

As with virtually all other components of the DWI process, many variables determine the duration of the arrest process. Factors that will affect the length include how long one has to wait for the tow truck, how far it is to the testing and/or booking facility, how long the driver opts to consult with an attorney, and how many extra forms there are due to civil processes. Generally, though, a DWI arrest usually takes two hours from stop to completion; on top of this, one can safely add another hour for the completion of all reports. The skilled officers who frequently arrest DWI suspects are often more proficient, and therefore their time commitment is less; in contrast, an officer who makes relatively few DWI arrests may take longer with the multiple reports and processes required with a DWI arrest.

The Training Officers Receive on DWI Procedures

With respect to the training that officers receive on DWI procedures, every state and agency is somewhat different. In Minnesota, we have peace officer licensing. Before law enforcement students are licensed, they are required to take Skills Training. In some professions, it would be called either practical training or basic training.

Most of the Skills Training courses are approximately eleven weeks long, three days of which are devoted to DWI enforcement. The NHTSA-approved SFST and Advanced SFST courses are taught to students by current or recently retired law enforcement officers.

Once the students are licensed and hired, some go directly to work; however, agencies such as ours run a separate academy. Our resident academy is four months long, and we devote more than a week of it to impaired driving enforcement. We spend two days covering law, court rulings, and agency policy. The students then go through the NHTSA-approved SFST and Advanced SFST courses. We also have a victims' impact panel where both offenders and victims come in to provide rookies with their experiences. The block of DWI instruction is concluded with officers participating in a mock court that involves an actual prosecutor and judge.

We provide legal updates monthly via e-mail so troopers are aware of current and changing case law and procedures in our state. As needed, we also provide refresher training in two- or three-hour blocks of instruction at our annual in-service training course. All sworn personnel from rookie to chief are required to attend the annual training.

The Most Important Steps When Testifying in Court

It should go without saying, but the most important thing for any peace officer when testifying is to be honest. It also helps to have a professional balance of confidence and humility, but honesty is the one element that is absolutely critical. If an officer is less than honest in any answer he or she gives, prosecutors and defense attorneys will realize it. Consequently, this reflects poorly on the officer, his or her agency, and any potential future good work the officer may do. A single breach of integrity by the officer may result in a cloud of suspicion that will cover that officer for years or even make them ineffective as a peace officer because of their tarnished reputation.

Officers preparing to testify in court should fully refresh their memory of the arrest by a complete review of their arrest reports. The officer should also focus on being professional. It may be necessary, or at least beneficial, to remember that having their actions and opinions attacked in a legal environment is part of their job and should not be taken personally. It is easy to feel unfairly attacked by the strategies of some defense attorneys; however, officers must remember the courtroom process is not a personal competition with defense counsel, but instead is a controlled environment for each side of an arrest to argue its position.

Officers should maintain a confident demeanor, but not a cocky one. Again, above all, they should be honest and unafraid to admit that they do not know or remember something, or that they are just not sure. Prior to the court hearing, officers should fully refresh themselves about the arrest by rereading the arrest report and compiling a copy or an abridged version of the report to refer to whenever they need to do so. Further, the officer should revisit the area where the arrest took place to clearly remember the roadway, terrain, and distinguishing features of the area.

The Most Common Attorney Mistakes in DWI Cases

Something I've seen some attorneys do that seems counterproductive is a mistake sometimes made by officers. They make the case personal. Officers and attorneys alike need to remember that this is part of a process and a system of checks and balances. When they become personally involved, they will interpret any challenging questions or answers as personal attacks and will be hard pressed to remain calm and objective.

In my opinion, the most effective defense attorneys are those who are respectful of the witnesses and focus on the issues or weaknesses of the arrest. Try as they may, attorneys seem less able to gain ground with anyone, including the jury, by being rude to or attacking the officer. Professional questions can just as easily reveal any shortcomings in the officer's work or reports without being dramatic or demeaning.

Common Misconceptions about How DWI Situations Are Handled by Law Enforcement Officials

One common misconception about handling DWI situations is that they are very simple, and there is really nothing substantial involved in the process: just stop a car at night and you probably will find an impaired driver. That is not the case at all. Even years ago, when DWI violations were more common, finding the offenders was not easy work. Currently, we will field a group of dedicated and talented officers to target DWI offenders; after seven or eight hours of patrol and stopping multiple vehicles, the officer may find that he or she has not identified a single impaired driver. In contrast, there are times when the officer will arrest two or three during that same shift.

Another misconception about officers making DWI arrests is that it is somehow enjoyable for them. While it is important work that helps reduce preventable crashes and the resulting serious injuries and deaths, it is hard work. It is an exhaustive process with little thanks.

Most of the people arrested for DWI are decent people. They have made an error in judgment and driven a motor vehicle after consuming too much alcohol. As stated above, judgment is one of the first things that alcohol affects, so it is quite possible—and actually a fairly frequent occurrence—that this violation is committed by otherwise good and decent citizens.

People who commit violent crimes, such as rape, robbery, or even burglary, against other persons have at the very least a reduced regard for the life, safety, and property of others. They intend to do harm at the cost of someone else. In contrast, though impaired drivers can do harm to others and even cause deaths that are horrifying, these are often otherwise good people who do not intend to harm others. The lack of good judgment and physical or mental impairment has made them a dangerous element on the highway system.

Sometimes citizens think that arresting combative and offensive DWI suspects is difficult. It is actually quite the opposite. In my experience, drivers who fight, swear, and spit on the officer are easy to arrest as compared to the driver who is honest and apologetic and admits that he or she has made a grave mistake. It is also challenging to make the arrest when the cooperative driver has children in the car. Those are the drivers I find the most difficult to arrest because I see how contritely they go through the process, and while I understand that this is necessary, it can be a heart-wrenching sight.

In my opinion, the greatest reminder to the patrol officer of the importance of DWI enforcement is the crashes that are caused by impaired drivers we didn't get to first. When an officer removes an injured or dead body from a vehicle in a crash caused by a drunken driver, it should serve as the clearest reminder that this is why we do what we do. Or when an officer makes a death notice in the middle of a night and watches as a family crumbles in his or her presence, those are the most defining moments as to the priority of DWI enforcement. After all, the crashes, injuries, and deaths that result from impaired driving are preventable!

Cases, Statutes, Regulations

Minnesota Statutes 169A.20 specifically, Chapter 169A (Minnesota Driving While Impaired Code) in general is relevant to the matters covered in this chapter. Here are the Web sites for it and its table of contents: https://www.revisor.leg.state.mn.us/statutes/?id=169A.20 and https://www.revisor.leg.state.mn.us/statutes/?id=169A.

Michael L. Asleson is a major with the Minnesota State Patrol. Major Asleson is a thirty-one year veteran with the patrol, receiving his initial training at the State Patrol Training Academy at Arden Hills in 1977. He has served at the State Patrol's West Metro, Detroit Lakes, and Mankato Districts. He currently serves in St. Paul, in charge of field operations.

Major Asleson is a 1988 graduate of Northwestern University's School of Police Staff and Command at Chicago. He is also a 1997 graduate of the FBI National Academy at Quantico, Virginia, and of the FBI Law Enforcement Executive Development Course.

A recipient of the Franklin M. Kreml Leadership Award, Major Asleson has been recognized by Mothers Against Drunk Driving and the Minnesota Insurance

Information Center for his contributions to DWI enforcement. He has instructed hundreds of Minnesota law enforcement officers in DWI detection and arrest skills and contributed to the creation of Minnesota's tiered DWI laws. He is a member of the Minnesota DWI Task Force and has regularly testified before the Minnesota Legislature and at legal conferences about DWI law and enforcement.

APPENDICES

Appendix A

MINNESOTA STATE PATROL DWI POLICY

GENERAL ORDER		
Effective: November 21, 2007*		**Number:** 07-70-007
Subject:	**DRIVING WHILE IMPAIRED (DWI)**	
Reference:	General Orders 20-028, 70-053, Minn. Statutes Chapter 169A, §609.21, 84.91-84.911, 86B.331-86B.335, 152.01, 169.01, 171.04, 171.09, 171.14, 171.16, 171.165, 171.166, 171.17, 171.18, 171.19, 171.30, 340A.503, 360.0752–360.0753, 626.556, Minnesota Rules 7409.2000, 7411.0100	
Special Instructions:	Rescinds General Orders 05-70-007, 05-30-020, 91-70-053; Supervisor Memos 03S-020, 02S-057; Trooper Memos 07-021, 07-001, 06-008, 04-026, 04-024, 04-002, 03-033, 03-025, 03-015, 03-014, 02-032, 94-020	**Distribution:** G

Revision Summary

*Pages 8 and 9 updated by Trooper Memo 08-008

I. POLICY

DWI offenders create a serious traffic safety threat. It is therefore the policy of the State Patrol to actively patrol and be vigilant for violations and driving conduct that may indicate alcohol/drug impairment and to strictly and aggressively enforce the offense of DWI. Troopers shall arrest any person suspected of being in violation of Minnesota's DWI laws.

II. INDEX

The remainder of this General Order is divided into the following sections:

III. DEFINITIONS

A. **Arrest Powers** (Minn. Statutes §169A.40 Subd. 1)

A peace officer may lawfully arrest a person for violation of Minn. Statutes §169A.20 (driving while impaired), §169A.31 (alcohol-related school bus or Head Start bus driving, or §169A.33 (underage drinking and driving), without a warrant upon probable cause, without regard to whether the violation was committed in the officer's presence.

B. **Driving While Impaired** (Minn. Statutes §169A.20)

Subdivision 1. **Driving while impaired crime.** It is a crime for any person to drive, operate, or be in physical control of any motor vehicle within this state or on any boundary water of this state:

1. When the person is under the influence of alcohol.

    Note: Court definition of "Under the Influence". *There is no set standard as to the quantity of alcohol a person must consume before a person is regarded as being "under the influence of alcohol." When a person is so affected by an alcoholic beverage that the person does not possess that clearness of intellect and control of himself/herself as he/she otherwise would have, that person is under the influence of alcohol. If a person consumes an alcoholic beverage and is not thereby influenced in the operation of his/her vehicle, there is no violation of the statute. If, however, as a result of consuming an alcoholic beverage, the person's ability or capacity to drive/operate/be in physical control of a motor vehicle is impaired, then the statute has been violated.*

2. When the person is *under the influence* of controlled substance. A controlled substance includes legal, prescription, and illegal drugs, including marijuana and tetrahydrocannabinols (Minn. Statutes §152.01, subd. 4).

3. When the person is *knowingly* under the influence of a hazardous substance (Minn. Rules 7411.0100 subp. 15) that affects the nervous system, brain, or muscles of the person so as to substantially impair the person's ability to drive or operate the motor vehicle.

4. When the person is under the influence of a combination of any two or more of the elements named in clauses (1), (2), and (3).

5. When the person's alcohol concentration *at the time*, or as measured within two hours of the time of driving, operating, or being in physical control of the motor vehicle, is 0.08 AC or more.

6. When the vehicle is a commercial motor vehicle and the person's alcohol concentration at the time, or as measured within two hours of the time of driving, operating, or being in physical control of the commercial motor vehicle, is 0.04 or more.

7. When the person's body contains *any amount* of a controlled substance listed in schedule I or II or its metabolite, other than marijuana or tetrahydrocannabinols. The mere presence of marijuana or tetrahydrocannabinols in a driver is not by itself sufficient. The driver must be under the influence of marijuana or THC and be charged under clause 2 above.

C. Aggravating Factors

1. Each prior DWI conviction or impaired driving-related loss of license within last 10 years, including prior offenses from other states (cannot count both if arising from the same incident);

2. Current test of 0.20 or over; or,

3. Child endangerment (less than 16 years of age and greater than 36 month difference from the offender).

D. Prior Impaired Driving Incident

Includes a prior conviction under the following Minn. Statutes:

Offense	Minnesota Statutes Section
Driving While Impaired	169A.20
Alcohol-Related School Bus or Head Start Bus Driving	169A.31
Impaired Aircraft Operation	360.0752
Criminal Vehicular Homicide and Operation, Substance Related Offenses	609.21 subdivision 1, clauses (2) to (6); 2006 Minnesota Statutes 609.21 subdivision 2, clauses (2) to (6); subdivision 2a, clauses (2) to (6); subdivision 2b, clauses (2) to (6);subdivision 3, clauses (2) to (6); or subdivision 4, clauses (2) to (6);

Driver Under the Influence of Alcohol or a Controlled Substance	169.121 (Minn. Statutes 1998)
Alcohol Related Driving by Commercial Vehicle Drivers	169.1211 (Minn. Statutes 1998)
Operating a Snowmobile, ATV, or Boat While Impaired	84.91, subdivision 1, paragraph (a), § 86B.331, subdivision 1, paragraph (a)
Driver's License Suspension, Revocation, Cancellation, Denial, or Disqualification because of an alcohol related incident	169A.31, 169A.50–169A.53, 169A.54, 171.04, 171.14, 171.16, 171.165, 171.17, 171.18, and 609.21; 169.123 (Minn. Statutes 1998)

An ordinance from this state, or a statute or ordinance from another state, in conformity with any provision listed above
A prior juvenile adjudication that would have been a prior impaired driving conviction if committed as an adult.
Also means the revocation of snowmobile or all terrain vehicle operating privileges under section 84.911 or motorboat operating privileges under section 86B.335 for violations that occurred *on or after August 1, 1995.*

IV. DWI: OFFENSES AND DEGREES

A. **First-Degree DWI—Felony** (Minn. Statutes §169A.24)

    1. A person is guilty of first-degree driving while impaired if the person is DWI and:

        a. commits the violation within ten years of the first of three or more qualified prior impaired driving incidents;

        b. has previously been convicted of a DWI felony under this statute; or

        c. has previously been convicted of felony criminal vehicular operation while impaired.

Note: Only prior offenses considered. Other aggravating factors are not applicable.

2. A person who commits first-degree driving while impaired is guilty of a felony and may be sentenced to imprisonment for not more than seven years, or to a payment of a fine of not more than $14,000, or both. The person is subject to the mandatory penalties described in Minn. Statutes §169A.276.

3. A person who violates this section requires mandatory booking, fingerprinting, and hold.

B. Second-Degree DWI—Gross Misdemeanor (Minn. Statutes §169A.25)

1. A person is guilty of second-degree driving while impaired if the person is DWI and two or more aggravating factors were present when the violation was committed.

2. A person who refuses to submit to a chemical test can be charged with second-degree driving while impaired if one aggravating factor was present when the violation was committed; however, most prosecutors choose to charge the refusal separately from the DWI charge (i.e., resulting in charges of 3rd degree DWI and gross misdemeanor refusal, with 2nd degree penalties). It is imperative that members understand the charging practices of their local prosecutors.

3. Second-degree driving while impaired is a gross misdemeanor. The mandatory penalties described in Minn. Statutes §169A.275 and the long term monitoring described in Minn. Statutes §169A.277 may be applicable.

4. A person who violates this section requires mandatory booking, fingerprinting, and hold.

C. Third-Degree DWI—Gross Misdemeanor (Minn. Statutes §169A.26)

1. A person is guilty of third-degree driving while impaired if the person is DWI and if one aggravating factor was present when the violation was committed.

2. A person who refuses to submit to a chemical test can be charged with third-degree driving while impaired; however, most prosecutors choose to charge the refusal separately from the DWI

charge (i.e., resulting in charges of 4th degree DWI and gross misdemeanor refusal, with 3rd degree penalties). It is imperative that members understand the charging practices of their local prosecutors.

3. Third-degree driving while impaired is a gross misdemeanor. The mandatory penalties described in Minn. Statutes §169A.275 and the long term monitoring described in Minn. Statutes §169A.277 may be applicable.

D. Fourth-Degree DWI—Misdemeanor (Minn. Statutes §169A.27)
1. A person is guilty of fourth-degree driving while impaired if they are DWI and no aggravating factors are present.
2. Fourth-degree driving while impaired is a misdemeanor.

E. Alcohol-Related School Bus or Head Start Bus Driving (Minn. Statutes §169A.31)
1. It is a crime for any person to drive, operate, or be in physical control of *any class of school bus or Head Start bus* within this state when there is physical evidence present in the person's body of the consumption of *any alcohol.*
2. A violation of this law is a gross misdemeanor if there is a person in the bus under the age of 16 and more than 36 months younger than the violator, or when the violator has a qualified prior impaired driving incident on their record. Any other violation is a misdemeanor.

V. DWI DETECTION

Troopers must be alert for signs of impairment due to alcohol, controlled substances, and/or hazardous substances in all contacts with motorists, making every effort to detect and apprehend impaired drivers. DWI detection and pre-arrest screening are the first steps in any DWI enforcement action. Troopers' observations during this stage are crucial in establishing probable cause upon which an arrest decision is based. Troopers should perform the following tasks:

A. Initial Observation/Stop/Face-to Face Contact

1. Recognize and identify specific driving behaviors that have a high probability of indicating that a driver may be under the influence of alcohol, controlled substance(s), and/or hazardous substance(s).
2. Exercise due care in pursuing impaired drivers and be prepared for unusual reactions from the driver.
3. Recognize and identify specific driving behavior during vehicle stops, which can provide additional evidence or suspicion that a driver may be impaired.
4. Note and document all observations leading to the suspicion that a driver may be impaired.
5. Approach vehicle with caution but with minimal delay.
6. Apprehend the driver as soon as possible and request assistance if needed.
7. Obtain the driver's license and other appropriate documents.
8. Interview the driver.
9. Do not allow a driver to move a vehicle once impairment is suspected.
10. Recognize and note specific characteristics, attitudes, and actions commonly observed in impaired drivers during this face-to-face contact. Troopers should be especially alert to the driver's ability to divide their attention.
11. If there are indications that the driver is impaired, request the driver to exit the vehicle for further investigation.
12. If the vehicle was not observed in motion, determine if probable cause exists to charge the driver with being in operation or physical control.
13. Accompany the driver to a safe location to conduct field sobriety tests.
14. All observations and actions of the driver must be documented in the Minnesota DWI Arrest Report and any supplemental report(s), to assist in the prosecution of the criminal case and in sustaining implied consent actions.

B. Field Sobriety Testing/Pre-Arrest Screening

1. When a Trooper detects possible impairment, the complete SFST battery shall be administered, unless it is not safe or practical to do so. The SFST battery *must* be administered in strict compliance

with testing procedures to serve as evidence of probable cause to arrest. If the SFST battery is not administered, the arresting trooper shall document the reason(s) why.

    a.   Field sobriety test results shall be recorded on the Minnesota State DWI Report. Troopers may also record initial SFST results on the pocket size SFST booklet (PS1827).

2.   A portable breath test (PBT) should be used by Troopers in conjunction with a DWI arrest. The PBT's sole purpose is to associate the driver's alcohol level with their level of impairment. The driver's impairment is determined primarily by SFSTs. The PBT is *only* used to corroborate alcohol as the causal factor of that impairment. Establishing impairment with SFSTs clearly rises to the level of specific, articulable facts that justify a PBT request required by case law (*Bladio v. Commissioner of Public Safety* and *State vs. Vievering*).

3.   If impairment is inconsistent with PBT results, Troopers should strongly consider the possibility of controlled substance(s), hazardous substance(s), and/or medical impairment. When controlled substance and/or hazardous substance impairment (e.g., little or no alcohol content, no nystagmus) is suspected, Troopers should request the assistance of a Drug Recognition Evaluator (DRE).

4.   The result of the PBT can also be used in the following court proceedings:

    a.   a civil action arising out of the operation or use of the motor vehicle;

    b.   an action for license reinstatement under Minn. Statutes §171.19;

    c.   a prosecution for a violation of Minn. Statutes §169A.20, subd. 2 (driving while impaired; test refusal);

    d.   a prosecution or juvenile court proceeding concerning a violation of Minn. Statutes §169A.33 (underage drinking and driving) or Minn. Statutes §340A.503 (underage alcohol consumption);

    e.   a prosecution under Minn. Statutes §169A.31 (alcohol-related school or Head Start bus driving) or Minn. Statutes §171.30 (limited license); or

f.   a prosecution for a violation of a restriction on a driver's license under Minn. Statutes §171.09, which provides that the license holder may not use or consume any amount of alcohol or a controlled substance (total abstinence restriction).

5.   When a suspect is impaired, an arrest should be made regardless of the results of the PBT or HGN test.

6.   The following policy will govern the use of the PBT following a motor vehicle collision resulting in property damage, personal injury, or death:

   a.   The Trooper will attempt to obtain both a screening test with the PBT and an evidentiary test pursuant to Minn. Statutes §169A.51 (see Section VI below) whenever they have probable cause to believe the driver is in violation of Minn. Statutes §169A.20.

   b.   In cases where probable cause exists that the driver is involved in a collision in violation of Minn. Statutes §169A.20 and is unable to perform SFSTs, the PBT should be utilized. If the driver provides a breath sample with a reading of .04 AC or greater or if the driver refuses to submit to the PBT, Troopers may invoke the ICA and obtain an evidentiary test. If the collision is likely to result in charges of Criminal Vehicular Homicide or Operation, refer to Section VII–E.

7.   The PBT must be operated in accordance with the guidelines set forth by the manufacturer and the BCA Breath Alcohol Section. PBTs must be checked for accuracy every two weeks to a ±.005 tolerance and calibrated when it falls out of tolerance. (See Addendum 1 for directions).

   a.   These checks must be documented on the PBT Accuracy Log. The last accuracy check/calibration shall be recorded on the Trooper's DWI Arrest Report. Maintaining the required log is essential for successful prosecution in DWI cases where a PBT was used to determine probably cause or as evidence in other cases.

   b.   Calibration and accuracy checks shall be completed using the simulator or dry gas solution only. Troopers should be aware of the number of simulator accuracy checks and calibration procedures run on each solution as it is recommended the solution can be used up to 25 times or 31 days before replacement.

VI. IMPLIED CONSENT/PEACE OFFICER'S

A. Implied Consent Advisory/Peace Officer's Certificate

1. The Implied Consent Advisory/Peace Officer Certificate form shall be completed for all persons believed to have driven, operated, or controlled a motor vehicle in violation of Minnesota DWI laws including criminal vehicular homicide and operation cases. This form is critical to the two-prong approach, which has proven so successful in dealing with the DWI problem. Test refusal is a crime; appropriate charges are to be filed.

2. The Implied Consent Advisory should be read prior to the Miranda warning. A driver must be provided a reasonable time to contact legal counsel for advice.

   a. There is no set standard for what length of time is "reasonable." The Trooper must look at the totality of the circumstances in determining when the test is being "unreasonably delayed." Giving a person 40 minutes may not be enough time under some circumstances, yet five minutes might be enough time in another case.

   b. As a general rule, when the person is making a good faith effort to obtain legal advice, they should be allowed to continue. However, when they have ceased their effort to contact an attorney or are no longer making forward progress, the limited right has been provided and the decision to test should be asked of the driver.

   c. While the person has the limited right to consult with an attorney, the current direction of the courts is to allow the person to call any person provided that call is made in an effort to ultimately reach an attorney (i.e., calling relative for the name/phone number of an attorney).

   d. A Trooper is not required to talk with the suspect's attorney or inform the suspect or their attorney of the digital PBT result.

3. Giving the Miranda warning to a suspect is mandatory prior to any in-custody questioning, but does not apply to the Implied Consent Advisory. It is important that the advisory portion be read verbatim from the form.

a. While not legally required by *Scales v. Minnesota*, it is the mandatory policy of the MSP that the reading of the Implied Consent Advisory be audio recorded. The arrest report must clearly indicate that an audio recording was made. Recording the reading of the advisory not only provides a good refresher and protection against unwarranted complaints for the Trooper called upon to testify in court, but also provides excellent evidence that can be used by the prosecutor and Attorney General in contested omnibus and revocation actions.

b. While a DWI suspect is talking with an attorney, the audio recording shall be discontinued; however, the member shall stay within close proximity to the suspect for security and breath test observation purposes. Any comments made by the suspect to the attorney are privileged and may not be used as evidence.

4. Commercial Vehicle Implied Consent Advisory should only be read for alcohol; read the standard motor vehicle advisory if presence of hazardous or controlled substances is suspected.

B. Chemical Testing

1. It is the policy of the State Patrol to request a breath test from a DWI suspect to the degree possible. The use of the Intoxilyzer expedites the judicial process and, in cases of tests above 0.08 (.04 if commercial vehicle), allows for immediate driver's license sanctions. The immediate impact on a person's driving privileges has proven to be an effective tool in preventing subsequent DWI offenses.

2. A member may request an evidentiary test when there is probable cause to believe the person was driving, operating, or in physical control of a motor vehicle in violation of Minn. Statutes §169A.20 and one of the following conditions exists:

a. The person has been lawfully placed under arrest for violation of Minn. Statutes §169A.20 or an ordinance in conformity with it.

b. The person has been involved in a motor vehicle crash or collision resulting in property damage, personal injury, or death.

    c. The person has refused to take the screening test provided for by Minn. Statutes §169A.20.

    d. The screening test was administered and indicated an alcohol concentration of .08 AC or more.

    e. The person was driving, operating, or in physical control of a commercial motor vehicle with the presence of any alcohol.

3. It is a crime for any person to refuse to submit to a chemical test of the person's blood, breath, or urine under Minn. Statutes §169A.20 subd. 2.

4. When a breath test is administered, a breath test consisting of two separate, adequate breath samples within .02 AC is acceptable. A breath test consisting of two separate, adequate breath samples failing to meet the .02 AC difference is deficient.

    a. If the first breath test is deficient, a second breath test must be administered.

    b. Two deficient breath tests constitute a refusal. Observations about the uncooperative suspect should be documented.

5. If offering a breath test is not possible or will adversely impact the arrest process and likelihood of a conviction, blood and/or urine test(s) may be pursued. The reason for deviation from this policy should be included in the Trooper's narrative report (examples: Intoxilyzer instrument not available, suspect's demonstrated inability to provide an adequate breath test, a PBT test showing an AC slightly above .08 that could become a test below .08 if not a deep lung sample).

6. After the suspect provides a chemical test or refuses testing, Troopers shall read the Miranda warning and ask the questions contained in the DWI packet. The audio recording of this portion of the processing phase is required by policy and Minnesota case law.

7. A blood or urine sample may be taken without consent from a person who is unconscious or otherwise unable to provide consent.

8. The Peace Officer's Certificate is used to report alcohol, hazardous substance, and controlled substance test results and refusals to the Commissioner of Public Safety. Tests over .08 (.04 for a commercial driver) will result in administrative driver's license

action. Tests of .07 or more shall also be reported for possible license action after repeated incidents

9. The Medical Personnel Certificate must be completed, even in the event that the ICA is not read, to record proper procedures in obtaining a blood test.

10. If a bodily fluid test is requested and the person refuses, an alternate test (which can include a breath test) must also be offered. If both blood and urine are offered at the outset and the driver chooses one but later refuses, then an alternative test need *not* be offered.

11. Blood/urine test results are to be recorded on paragraph #9 of the Peace Officer's Certificate by the Trooper *after* they are received in the district office. The Trooper shall sign and date the POC to certify the test results only after they are received.

12. When a Trooper obtains a breath sample and the test result reveals a low alcohol concentration (as compared to the degree of impairment), the Trooper shall consider that the impairment is due to controlled substances and/or hazardous substances other than alcohol.

13. Troopers must ensure that the person obtaining the test, the blood/urine kit number, member's District Office number, and date/time of test are recorded on the blood/urine kit card and within the narrative arrest report.

14. Blood/urine kits will be kept at the BCA for a period of six months from the last lab report for each specific kit. If members need the evidence for a longer period of time, they should email bca.lab@state.mn.us and the kit will be sent to the DPS warehouse.

C. Second Test for Controlled Substance

1. Minn. Statutes §169A.51 subd. 4 provides that a blood or urine test may be required even after a breath test has been administered if there is probable cause to believe that there is impairment by a controlled substance or hazardous substance that is not subject to testing by a breath test, or a controlled substance listed in schedule I or II or its metabolite, other than marijuana or tetrahydrocannabinols, is present in the person's body.

a. Action may be taken against a person who refuses to take a blood test under this subdivision only if a urine test was offered, and action may be taken against a person who refuses to take a urine test only if a blood test was offered. The Trooper does not have to offer the test options at the same time.

2. A second ICA should be completed and read before a second test is requested, unless the Trooper read both the alcohol and controlled substance portions of the ICA initially, in which case the second test can merely be requested without the additional reading.

D. Additional Testing

1. The person has the right to have someone of their own choosing administer a chemical test or tests in addition to any administered at the direction of a peace officer, provided that the additional test sample on behalf of the person is obtained at the place where the person is in custody, after the test administered at the direction of a peace officer, and at no expense to the state.

2. Troopers do not need to inform the driver of this right, however, if an additional test is requested, a telephone and telephone books must be made available. The Trooper need not take the time/expense to transport the person to a different facility (i.e., hospital) for purposes of an additional test.

VII. SPECIAL CIRCUMSTANCES

A. Uncooperative Driver

1. A Trooper should first ask a driver to perform simple tests (reciting alphabet, counting backwards, a finger count) while they remain in their vehicle. If the driver is uncooperative, Troopers may request that a driver exit their vehicle. The Trooper should establish other indicia of intoxication (eyes, odor, dexterity, coordination, etc.) and attempt to have the driver expressly refuse to exit and perform SFSTs. A video and/or audio recording of the event are helpful in these situations to document the event.

2. The Trooper can then make a request of the driver to submit to the PBT while still seated in their vehicle. The multiple refusals of the driver will prove helpful in later proving that the driver was

impaired, and that the evasive conduct was done to avoid detection.

B. Commercial Vehicle Operators

The per se limit for operators of commercial vehicles is 0.04. Persons with an AC of .04 may not display visible signs of impairment. Therefore, the driver of a commercial vehicle that displays any detectable presence of an alcoholic beverage in their body should be requested to provide a PBT. If the PBT is refused or displays and AC of .04 or greater, the Commercial Vehicle Implied Consent Advisory should be invoked.

C. DWI Without Witnessing Driving

Troopers investigating crashes or checking disabled/stalled vehicles containing DWI suspects should thoroughly investigate the elements of the crime, including the time of driving/operation/physical control, and whether there is any claim of post-crash/driving consumption. Questions contained within the DWI Arrest Report are designed to confront such a claim.

D. Driving Complaints

An anonymous report of an impaired driver is *not* sufficient in and of itself to justify a lawful stop. Similarly, any report of an impaired driver which lacks information as to the basis for the caller's mere conclusion that a driver is impaired is not sufficient in and of itself to justify a lawful stop. Under these circumstances where specifics are not provided, members need to establish reasonable suspicion to stop a vehicle based on their own observations.

E. Criminal Vehicular Operation and Homicide

1. Troopers shall not_invoke the Implied Consent Advisory (ICA) and read the advisory to drivers suspected of alcohol or drug-related criminal vehicular homicide or injury violations. Instead, a test may be administered without regard to the suspect's consent or refusal as the "rapid, natural dissipation of alcohol in the blood" can be considered an exigent circumstance (*State v. Shriner, 2008, Minn*).

2. When a test is obtained from a conscious driver suspected of being in violation of vehicular homicide or injury, no ICA is read and therefore no Peace Officer's Certificate or ICA should be completed. Nevertheless, troopers must ensure that the person obtaining the test, the blood/urine kit number, and date/time of test are recorded on the blood/urine kit card and within the narrative arrest report.

3. Pursuant to Minn. Rule 7409.2000, a suspect charged with criminal vehicular operation or homicide may have their license immediately suspended prior to a hearing based upon the issuance of a complaint against them. District Commanders are responsible to ensure that a copy of the formal complaint for any count(s) of criminal vehicular homicide or operation is submitted to DPS Driver and Vehicle Services so action can be taken against the suspect's driving privileges.

F. Underage Drinking and Driving

Minn. Statutes §169A.33 covers the crime of underage drinking by the driver of a vehicle (less than 21 years of age). This law, also referred to as Minnesota's "Not a Drop" law is an underage consumption charge specifically reserved for motor vehicle drivers/operators/persons in physical control of a motor vehicle. *It is not a replacement for the charge of DWI* and should be enforced when there is evidence the driver consumed an alcoholic beverage but is not impaired. Convictions under this law cannot be used as an aggravating factor for enhancing future DWI violations.

G. Reporting Student Drug and/or Alcohol Violations

Minn. Statutes §121A.28 requires law enforcement agencies to provide written notice of any drug incident involving a student to the student's chemical abuse pre-assessment team. This notice is to be provided to the chemical abuse pre-assessment team within two weeks of the incident. The Trooper is responsible for identifying the school that the student attends and then providing this notice, either through the Field Report or through a written statement to the student's chemical abuse pre-assessment team.

H. Off-Road Recreational Vehicles or Motorboat

Off-road recreational vehicles and motorboats are covered under Minn. Statutes §169A.07 with references to Minn. Statutes §84.91–84.911; boats are referenced under Minn. Statutes §86B.331–86B.335. The provisions closely parallel the motor vehicle DWI statutes except that the first offense on an off-road vehicle or motorboat is treated differently than second or subsequent offenses. Testing is mandatory (misdemeanor) and revocation of operating privileges for refusal. Forms for enforcing DWI of off-road recreational vehicle and motorboat laws are available in complete packets from Conservation Officers. District Offices should obtain a supply of these packets from the DNR.

I. Aircraft

Aircraft are covered under Minn. Statutes §360.0752–360.0753. These statutes also closely parallel the motor vehicle law but there are no special forms. In the event a member makes an arrest for operating an aircraft while under the influence, the advisory should be read from the statute.

J. Limited Driver's License

1. When a driver violates the driver's license restriction of "any use of alcohol or drugs invalidates license," the correct charge is VIOLATE LIMITED DRIVER'S LICENSE Minn. Statutes §171.09. The driver's license status does not automatically revert back to their invalid status (i.e., revoked).

2. Whenever a Trooper knows of a total abstinence restriction violation, such as "any use of alcohol or drugs invalidates license," a memo and narrative reports shall be sent via the District Office to the Department of Public Safety, Driver and Vehicle Services, Attention Chief Driver Evaluator. The narrative report should include detailed observations of alcohol use. Every effort should be made to obtain a PBT result.

3. This requirement applies whether or not the person is driving. The restriction from the use of alcohol or drugs is part of their mandatory rehabilitation and total abstinence is required to maintain a driving privilege.

K. Child Endangerment

1. Minn. Statutes §626.556 subd. 2(b) defines "neglect" as "…failure to protect a child from conditions or actions which imminently and seriously endanger the child's physical or mental health when reasonably able to do so…"

2. When a driver is arrested for DWI involving "child endangerment," the District Office will send a copy of the Arrest Report to the county social services/child protection agency in the county where the violation occurred. This procedure applies whether or not the driver is the parent of the child. "Child" is defined as any person under the age of 18.

L. Affirmative Defense—Alcohol (Post-Driving Consumption)

Minn. Statutes §169A.46, subdivision 1 provides for the introduction of evidence at the evidentiary hearing that consumption occurred after driving/arrest. Troopers who do not observe the driving conduct of a DWI suspect (i.e., crash scene) should investigate any claims of after driving consumption. This can be accomplished by asking questions at the scene prior to the arrest, and also asking questions contained within the DWI form following the reading of the Miranda warning. Further, Troopers should ask about the location of containers when any post driving consumption is claimed.

M. Affirmative Defense—Prescription Drug

1. It is a violation to drive under the influence of any controlled substance, even one that is prescribed, regardless if it is taken within the terms of the prescription. However, Minn. Statutes §169A.46 subd. 2 provides that a person charged with having *only the presence* of a schedule I or II controlled substance (and not under the influence of it) has not violated Minn. Statutes §169A.20 subd. 1, clause 7 (presence of schedule I or II controlled substance) *if the prescription has been taken within the terms of the prescription.*

2. Troopers arresting a driver for DWI controlled substance should ask questions from the DWI packet (following Miranda) regarding any prescription drugs, including the name of the substance, dosage, quantity and time taken. It is also important to examine the prescriptions, if possible, to determine whether the drug prescription prohibited driving and/or using in combination with alcohol.

VIII. BOOKING & DISPOSITION

A. Booking

1. Persons arrested for DWI should be booked in the appropriate jail.

2. 36 hour rule. Troopers booking DWI suspects to be held pending charging by formal complaint must be alert to the 36 hour rule. The 36 hours starts at 0001 hours the day following the arrest. Sundays and holidays are excluded from the time calculation. The arresting Trooper is responsible for getting a complete arrest report and supplemental documents to the responsible prosecutor so charging can occur before expiration of the 36 hours (see General Order 20-028 Arrest, Hold, Incarceration, Release from Custody).

3. 48 hour rule. Troopers booking DWI suspects to be held pending charging by formal complaint must be alert to the 48 hour Probable Cause Rule. The 48 hours starts at the time of arrest. All days (including the day of arrest, Sundays, and legal holidays) *are* included in the time calculation. A summary of the arrest must be sent to the appropriate judge for a probable cause hold review. No prisoner can be held beyond the 48 hour limit without the judge's approval/order. Further, no prisoner may be held beyond the time a judge is available to review the probable cause for arrest (see General Order 20-028 (Arrest, Hold, Incarceration, Release from Custody)).

   a. The arresting Trooper is responsible for providing a summary of the arrest to the prosecutor or judge for this purpose. Troopers may provide a full arrest report, or shall make a copy of the Minnesota State DWI Report for this purpose, since only limited information is needed for the probable cause hold review.

   b. Some County Attorneys request that the hold request go through them and then to the judge. Troopers shall follow the request of their local prosecutor.

   c. While 48 hours is allowed for this process, Troopers must provide the required paperwork in a timely fashion to avoid the unwanted release of a prisoner well before expiration of the 48 hours.

   Example: Some larger counties have a judge responsible for doing probable cause hearings on a daily basis—including weekends. A suspect booked at 0200 hours may go before the judge at 0900 hours that same date. Even though the 48 hours has not expired, a judge is available, and the suspect could be released if the judge does not have the proper paperwork.

B. Other Accommodations

1. Where the local sheriff has adopted a policy of not accepting State Patrol DWI prisoners or there is no room at the booking facility, the DWI suspect may be taken to a detox facility.

2. When the jail facility is not available, and there is no detox facility within a reasonable distance that would accept the prisoner, Troopers may release the prisoner to a sober adult who agrees to take charge of the suspect. Troopers should record the name and address of the sober adult they release the suspect to in their report.

IX. ADMINISTRATIVE & CIVIL ACTIONS

A. Driver's License

1. Notice and Order of Revocation/Temporary Driver's License, *Non*-Commercial Driver

   a. If a subject refuses a chemical test, or submits to a breath test indicating an alcohol concentration of .08 AC percent or more, issue the Notice and Order of Revocation.

   b. If the subject is a *Minnesota licensed driver*, invalidate the driver's license by clipping the   license at the lower right corner without obscuring any pertinent information and return it to the driver with a Notice and Order of Revocation/Temporary Driver's License form.

   c. Issue the temporary license if satisfied with a positive identification.

   d. Do not issue the Notice and Order of Revocation or temporary driver's license to subjects submitting to blood or urine tests. Administrative action will be taken by DVS upon receipt of test results.

2. Notice and Order of *Commercial* Driver Revocation/Disqualification

   a. The operator of a commercial vehicle with any amount of alcohol (including less than 0.04 AC) is in violation and shall be advised they are out of service for 24 hours. The warning form (1801) or the truck inspection form may be used to record the out of service order.

b. If the driver of a commercial vehicle provides an evidentiary test *between* .04 AC and .08 AC, the member should service them with the Commercial Driver Disqualification.

c. If the driver of the commercial vehicle provides an evidentiary test *over* .08 AC, the member should serve them with both the motor vehicle Notice of Revocation and the Notice and Order of *Commercial* Driver Revocation/Disqualification, The appropriate advisory box is to be checked and, in the case of a Minnesota licensed driver, the license is to be invalidated.

B. License Plate Impoundment (Minn. Statutes § 169A.60)

1. Only Minnesota motor vehicle license plates can be impounded. Pursuant to Minn. Statutes §169A.60, motor vehicle license plates may be impounded under the following factors:

   a. DWI plus one aggravating factor (or related offense from another state within 10 years); or

   b. Violator is cancelled inimical to public safety (DWI or sober).

2. Serve a Notice and Order of License Impoundment, except for when blood or urine tests are requested which will result in administrative revocation by DVS upon receipt of test results.

   a. If the violator is the owner of the vehicle, circle the "7" day on the temporary permit.

   b. If the driver is not the owner, circle the "45" day on the temporary permit.

   c. Instruct the owner or driver to place the "Vehicle Copy" of the temporary permit in the rear window of the vehicle before it is operated.

3. Seize the plates of vehicle violator is currently driving, regardless of ownership.

   a. Notify the owner/violator that all plates issued them must be turned into a law enforcement agency within seven days, and refer the owner to the appeal procedures on the back side of form PS 2485-01.

   b. Forward the seized plates and the department and agency copies of form PS2486-01 to the District Office.

    c.   Troopers who encounter a vehicle that lists the license plates as "revoked for alcohol" should seize and destroy the plates. A Notice and Order of License Plate Impoundment s*hould not* be issued in these cases.

C.   Vehicle Forfeiture (Minn. Statutes §169A.63, subd. 2)

  1.   A vehicle may be seized subject to forfeiture when the seizure is incident to a lawful arrest of the owner or of another person, if the owner or lessor knew or should have known of the violation, for a designated offense which includes an arrest for DWI or an aggravated offense or another statute or ordinance in conformance with these:

    a.   1st degree felony DWI;

    b.   2nd degree gross misdemeanor DWI;

    c.   3rd degree DWI arrest with a test refusal

    d.   DWI or refusal violation with a cancel-inimical to public safety (IPS) status; or

    e.   DWI or refusal, violation with a total abstinence ("B card") license restriction.

  2.   The owner of a motor vehicle is a "person who legally has possession, use, and control of the motor vehicle, including a lessee, for 180 days or more." Frequently the actual owner is different from the registered owner because the title has not been transferred on the vehicle, or the vehicle was registered to a friend or relative who furnished the vehicle to the defendant for their long-term use. To prevail in court, a member must be able to prove that the vehicle is actually owned and operated by the defendant and not the registered owner, so members should question the driver about their use of the vehicle, examine all records in the vehicle, call the registered owner, etc.

  3.   The clear intent of the vehicle forfeiture law pertaining to DWI is to remove the availability of a motor vehicle from use by the impaired operator. Additionally, the legislature clearly intended for all vehicles seized within the criteria for vehicle forfeiture to be forfeited.

  4.   It is the policy of the Minnesota State Patrol to seize and initiate forfeiture proceedings on *all* motor vehicles meeting the criteria of

the vehicle forfeiture provisions of Minn. Statutes §169A.63. Use the [copyrighted] Minnesota County Attorney Association Form.

5. Each county attorney having jurisdiction within a State Patrol district is responsible for determining how the vehicle is to be processed after the initial seizure. In *all* cases, determination shall be made after consultation with the corresponding county attorney, if the seized motor vehicle is to be forfeited or released. This determination is to be made as soon as possible following the arrest.

6. Forfeiture Procedures

   a. A vehicle used in the above offenses should be taken into custody in appropriate cases. Follow the procedures prescribed in General Order 80-005 (Forfeitures of Property).

   b. If used, a towing company *must* be advised that the State Patrol is not liable for any storage fees.

   c. Reasonable steps must be taken to secure the vehicle and prevent damage.

   d. The prosecuting attorney should be advised when a vehicle is seized subject to forfeiture.

   e. Forfeiture can only take place after conviction of the original charge.

   f. If the court orders forfeiture of a vehicle, it may order the vehicle sold or used by the agency.

   g. The Chief, or his/her designee, should be contacted for a decision whether the court should be asked to order the vehicle to be used by the State Patrol.

   h. If the vehicle is given to the agency, it will be assigned by the Fleet and Supply Manager.

   i. If the vehicle is ordered sold, all liens, sale expenses, and storage costs must be paid from the proceeds.

X. REPORTING REQUIREMENTS

A. DWI Arrest Report

Use of the MSP DWI Arrest Report (form PS1812A-09) is mandatory for all DWI arrests and Criminal Vehicular Operation investigations involving impairment of any substance.

1. The arrest report should contain all observations that caused the Trooper to have reasonable suspicion to make the traffic stop and

probable cause to make the DWI arrest. The Trooper's arrest report shall indicate the existence of any and all audio or video recordings.

B. Miranda Warning/DWI Report Packet

Following the chemical testing process (or refusal), Troopers shall read the DWI suspect the Miranda warning and ask questions from the DWI report packet. (Reminder: The Miranda warning as well as the questions/answers/refusal to answer shall be audio recorded.)

C. Charging

When permitted by the local court, a uniform traffic citation (form 1821) shall be issued for the DWI offense and other charge(s). When the use of a traffic citation is not possible, the charge should be carried out through a tab charge or formal complaint. Troopers shall document the charge(s) listed on the tab charge or contained in the formal complaint on the goldenrod copy of form 1821.

1.   Only one DWI arrest code should be recorded for each DWI arrest. Even in those cases where the prosecutor contains multiple DWI counts in the formal complaint or requires the Trooper to list counts separately, only one DWI code may be used.

2.   Members charging a driver for an alcohol-related Criminal Vehicular Operation or Homicide offense shall record the CVO charge and also the DWI offense on the 1821 form and enter the offenses onto the weekly report form.

     Example: DWI arrest. 1 Aggravating Factor. Over .08 test.

     Charge: 3rd Degree DWI (Gross Misdemeanor)

     169A.20 Subd. 1 (1) Under Influence Alcohol

     169A.20 Subd. 1 (5) Over .08

     169A.26 3rd Degree (Gross Misd.) DWI

     Claim 3rd Degree DWI, Code 1063 only.

3.   Troopers should not cite drivers with moving violations that were part of the Trooper's basis for making the DWI arrest (i.e., speed, over center line, failure to dim, etc.). Likewise, Troopers shall not take activity for such offenses. Other offenses observed that are not a basis for the stop should, however, be cited (i.e., driver's license violations, refusal to test, equipment offenses, open bottle, drug offenses).

D. Drug Recognition Evaluator

When a DRE (Drug Recognition Evaluator) is asked to assist with a DWI arrest, only the arresting Trooper should record the arrest on their weekly report form. DREs are required to complete a *Drug Influence Evaluation* face sheet as well as a narrative report detailing their observations, and forward the reports to the State DRE Coordinator.

E. Forms

A non-inclusive list of forms to be completed and submitted to the district office in connection with a DWI arrest follows. It is essential that all required forms be submitted without delay. It is especially critical that the Peace Officer's Certificate, Notice of Intent to Revoke, and Commercial Driver Disqualification forms be received by Driver and Vehicle Services within seven days of the incident.

1. MN State DWI Report (1812A-09) and supplemental arrest narrative
2. Motor Vehicle Implied Consent Advisory/Peace Officer Certificate (1802)
3. Vehicle in Custody Report (1818)
4. Intoxilyzer Test Record (50591)
5. Uniform Traffic Ticket (1821)
6. Notice and Order of Revocation/Temporary Driver's License (31123)
7. Notice and Order of Revocation and/or Disqualification (31124) (commercial drivers only)
8. Notice and Order of License Plate Impoundment (2486)
9. Commercial Vehicle Implied Consent Advisory/Peace Officer Certificate (1817)
10. Offender Tracking Form (OTF)
11. Off-road/recreational vehicle/motorboat report forms

XI. RESPONSIBILITIES

A. Member

1. Complete all reports and forms required in the DWI arrest as soon as practical following the arrest.

2. Ensure that all observations, evidence, factual information, witness information (local police officers, jailers who witnessed the tests being administered, and citizens who reported the DWI suspect), and appropriate opinions are contained in the reports.

    a. Request a copy of the audio 911 call from the Radio Communications Operators if a witness called in to report a driving complaint that resulted in a DWI arrest.

3. Complete an Offender Tracking Form for each person arrested for DWI.

4. Submit reports to prosecutor directly or via district office, as circumstances and local procedures dictate.

5. Maintain all audio/video tapes until the matter has been adjudicated, including the Implied Consent hearing.

6. Provide written notice as required in Minn. Statutes §121A.28 within two weeks of the offense to the student's school chemical abuse pre-assessment team.

B. District/Section Commander

1. Review arrest and related reports to ensure that the arrests have been made according to MSP policy and are thoroughly documented.

2. Ensure dictated arrests are transcribed and copies are sent to appropriate prosecutors.

3. Send the Peace Officer's Certificate and all accompanying reports to Driver and Vehicle Services, Implied Consent Section.

4. Send a copy of any arrest report involving DWI Child Endangerment to the appropriate social services agency in the county of occurrence.

5. Forward License Plate Impoundment and Vehicle Forfeiture forms to Driver and Vehicle Services and appropriate prosecutors.

    a. Develop a logging system to keep up-to-date records of all impounded license plates, whether turned in by a Trooper or delivered to the office by an owner.

    b. Immediately forward the department copy of the Notice and Order of License Plate Impoundment to the Central Office for forwarding to Driver and Vehicle Services.

    c. Ensure that all impounded plates are destroyed.

    d. After the plates are destroyed, send a photocopy of the impoundment order to the Central Office for forwarding to DVS.

  6. Contact the BCA (tony.petracca@state.mn.us) to set up prosecutor access to online DWI tests, or provide paper copies of the test results to prosecutors.

C. Radio Communications Operators

1. Obtain pertinent information from a citizen reporting a suspected DWI, such as the name, address, and home and work telephone numbers of the citizen making the report.
2. Determine why the complainant believes the suspect is impaired, and/or what driving conduct has been observed.
3. Provide a summary of the information collected to the Investigating Member.

Approved: **Signed 11/21/2007** _____ **Colonel Mark A. Dunaski, Chief** **Minnesota State Patrol**	**I have read and understand this General Order.** _____ **Signature**

Addendum 1	Number: 07-16-016

OPERATION, CALIBRATION, AND ACCURACY CHECKS FOR THE ALCO-SENSOR IV

I. OPERATION OF ALCO-SENSOR IV

A. Operating Conditions

1. The Alco-Sensor IV is designed to operate at instrument temperatures between 50 degrees F (10 degrees, Celsius) to 104 degrees F. (40 degrees, Celsius); Tests can be run every two minutes. Temperature is important as the rate of the electro-chemical reaction is affected by temperature.

2. Once the unit is at operating temperature it will function properly in ambient temps of 0 degrees C to 40 degrees C and relative humidity of 0 to 100%.

3. The instrument's temperature is displayed when the mouthpiece is mounted. If, it is below 10 degrees C or above 40 degrees C, the test is blocked. Remove the mouthpiece and place the unit somewhere that the temperature can adjust to an acceptable operating temperature. It will come to an acceptable operating temperature in a short period of time.

B. Interfering Substances

The Alco-Sensor IV responds to alcohol in the breath. It does NOT read acetone or hydrocarbons which might be found in the breath.

C. Fuel Cell Clean-Up

Sufficient time after each test must be allowed for all traces of alcohol on the cell surface to be eliminated. If the Alco-Sensor IV is ready for use, the output of the fuel cell will be stable zero and the display will indicate this state by calling for a blank. Even when exposed to breath samples with moderate to high alcohol levels (>.040), a cell should clear within two minutes. Keeping the unit warm will speed this process. At least one minute should elapse after a positive test result which is greater than .000 and <.040 before another test sequence is initiated.

D. Radio Frequency Interference

An RFI sensor is built into the Alco-Sensor IV's circuitry. If an interference signal is received which could influence the test result, the test will be voided and "RFI" will be displayed. No result will be available. The test will have to be started over by removing the mouthpiece to turn the unit off. A possible source of RFI can be keying the portable radio.

E. Procedure for Conducting a Breath Test with Alco-Sensor IV

If the Alco-Sensor IV is being used as a screening test, the subject should be asked if they have drunk or used alcohol or smoked in the last 15 minutes. If the response is negative, test the subject immediately; if otherwise or a foreign object is found in their mouth, wait 15–20 minutes for alcohol and five minutes for a foreign object or smoking before testing. Always check the subject's mouth before testing.

F. Operating Instructions

1. Mount a NEW mouthpiece to unit—unit turns on.
2. Note the temperature displayed.
3. If the unit displays "SET", depress Set button. When the unit displays "BLANK", the unit runs BLANK automatically and displays ".000"(*).
4. If the unit displays "SET", depress the Set button.
5. When the unit displays "TEST", collect a breath sample by using the Manual Capture function.
6. Note the three digit reading.
7. Depress Set button and remove the mouthpiece.

G. Recalling the Current Test Result

Until the Set button is depressed after a test, the RECALL function is not available. Once the Set button has been engaged, depressing the recall button will display the final reading of the current test. After the mouthpiece is ejected, the test result cannot be recalled.

H. Accuracy Checks

Accuracy checks can be completed using either the Simulator Solution attached to an Intoxilyzer or with the dry gas tanks provided in all station offices. If the Simulator Solution is used, follow instructions 1–5. If the dry gas tank is used, follow instructions 6–9.

1. Prepare simulator for use and be sure it has reached a stable temperature (34 degrees C) and that the stirrer is operating properly.

2. Prepare the PBT the same as when obtaining a sample from a driver. When the Alco-Sensor IV reaches "TEST", attach open end of mouthpiece to simulator outlet.

3. Blow into simulator inlet port for approx. four seconds. Avoid blowing so hard that solution is aspirated into the Alco-Sensor IV mouthpiece. On approximately the third second, press the Manual button on Alco-Sensor IV to take a sample. (The goal is to have gas still flowing through the Alco-Sensor IV when the sample is taken).

4. Detach simulator from mouthpiece carefully so that the mouthpiece is not unseated from the unit.

5. Record reading. If it does not correspond to the expected value (the actual certified simulator reading), the unit needs calibration.

6. Prepare the PBT the same as when obtaining a sample from a driver. When the Alco-Sensor IV reaches "TEST", attach open end of mouthpiece to dry gas tank outlet on the regulator.

7. Depress the button on the top of the regulator to dispel gas. Hold the button down for 4 seconds. On the third second, press the Manual button on Alco-Sensor IV to capture a sample.

8. Detach tank from mouthpiece carefully so that the mouthpiece is not unseated from the unit.

9. Record reading. If it does not correspond to the expected value (as listed on the tank), the unit needs calibration.

I. Calibration

When a unit does not read a simulator or dry gas solution within acceptable limits (±.005), it must be calibrated by the following procedure. The unit must be calibrated when its temperature is between 23 degrees to 27 degrees C. If the temperature is not within the required range, the unit will not permit a calibration.

1. Remove battery cover to expose calibration switch access holes.

2. Insert a NEW mouthpiece and follow standard operation until Alco-Sensor IV displays a blank reading of ".000".

3. While ".000" is still being displayed, press Access Hole #3 and hold down until ".XXX" is displayed (The actual number will be that used for the last calibration that was run). When ".XXX" display appears, release button. If the temperature is not in the range of 23 degrees to 27 degrees C, instead of ".XXX" the display will be "TMP>" or

"TMP<" and the unit will "VOID". Remove the mouthpiece and correct temperature before trying again.

4. If, after a few seconds, the display goes to "SET", the Set button should be depressed to cock the sample pump. ".XXX" will return to the display.

5. With ".XXX" shown on the display, adjust the number up (Access Hole #1) or down (Access Hole #2) until the value of the simulator or dry gas solution being used is displayed.

6. Push Access Hole #3 again and display will read "CAL". This is the equivalent of "TEST" in a normal sequence.

7. Connect unit to simulator or dry gas tank. Introduce a sample using the same procedure listed in section 3 or 7 of the Accuracy Check (above). The microprocessor will analyze the output from the fuel cell and will automatically accept the number that was programmed in Step 5.

8. Conclude the test as usual by pressing the Set button when "Set" appears. Remove the mouthpiece at the intermittent BEEP. The conversion factors that were calculated in Step 7 are preserved in the Alco-Sensor, IV memory and are used for every test until a new set is computed by a subsequent calibration.

9. After a two minute wait, use a new mouthpiece to run an Accuracy Check test with the same simulator or dry gas solution to confirm the calibration. It should be within ±.005 of the target reading.

10. Any calibration questions should be directed to the BCA Breath Alcohol Section at 651/793-2781.

11. The life of the fuel cell of the PBT is dependant on moisture. A fuel cell that regularly has a breath sample introduced into it will 'live' longer than one that does not. With the advent of the dry gas for calibration, some PBTs do no get adequate moisture across the fuel cell. It is recommended that when Troopers are finished with their bi-monthly calibration check, they introduce a breath sample into their PBT to insure adequate moisture on the fuel cell.

Courtesy of Major Michael L. Asleson, Minnesota State Patrol

Appendix B

MINNESOTA STATE PATROL DWI ARREST REPORT

MINNESOTA STATE PATROL
DWI ARREST REPORT - SUPPLEMENTAL

CASE CONTROL NUMBER:	
DEFENDANT:	
DATE OF BIRTH: Check of Juvenile ☐	
DATE OF ARREST:	

PRELIMINARY:

List any preliminary information not already contained on other pages of the DWI packet, such as special weather or traffic conditions, assignment (i.e., Night-CAP), civilian rider, field training trooper present, etc.

INITIAL OBSERVATION:

List first observations of what drew your attention to the offender and their actions; driving behavior, crash scene, citizen complaint, stalled vehicle, etc. Articulate what reasonable suspicion(s) lead to the decision to stop the vehicle.

STOP:

List actions/observations that occurred during stop; unusual actions taken, offender's response to stop command, method(s) used to signal stop command, any observed attempts to hide contraband/weapons, the fashion in which offender stopped the vehicle.

FACE-TO-FACE CONTACT:

List appearance, eyes, speech, pupils, passenger info, unusual actions/statements; what you saw/heard/smelled, & other observations. If needed, how you established driving/operation/physical control. List pre arrest admissions/statements. How driver ID'd?.

PRE-ARREST SCREENING (SFST's/PBT):

Describe exit and unusual actions. Describe physical/mental performance during SFSTs. Describe any refusal to perform and any disabilities that would prevent performance. PBT Given? PBT result and last date of accuracy check.

ARREST:

Entire basis for probable cause to arrest listed here, or earlier in report. Define when offender was advised of arrest. Disposition of veh., keys, passengers, & property. Transportation & arrival times, mouth checks, & voluntary admissions/statements.

IMPLIED CONSENT/TESTING:

Info about reading of Advisory or why not read. Info beyond Advisory (attempts to contact attorney, cooperation, admissions). Test type, time, where taken, administered by whom. Your actions if 2nd test requested. Note chain of custody of test sample(s).

MIRANDA/STATEMENT:

List any comments not already contained on the questionnaire page of the DWI arrest report.

FINAL DISPOSITION:

Where was the offender taken? List any information about holds, pending charges and any information about the booking or release not already contained elsewhere in the DWI arrest report.

MISC.:

List information about arrest not already in DWI arrest report. What forms given to offender (i.e., Notice of Revocation, Lic. Plate Impoundment, Veh. Forfeiture, Intoxilyzer Test Record). If applicable, list/attach the offenders driving record.

CHARGES:

What was the offender charged with? Or, what charges do you recommend for prosecution via formal complaint.

Signature:	
Arresting Trooper:	DATE:

Courtesy of Major Michael L. Asleson, Minnesota State Patrol

Appendix C

MOTOR VEHICLE IMPLIED CONSENT ADVISORY

ICR
MOTOR VEHICLE
IMPLIED CONSENT ADVISORY

Time Started _____

Location read: _____

_____ ,
(person arrested)

I believe you have been driving, operating, or controlling a motor vehicle in violation of Minnesota's D.W.I. laws and "you have been placed under arrest for this offense" or "you have been involved in a motor vehicle accident resulting in property damage, personal injury, or death."

_____ 1.   Minnesota law requires you to take a test to determine:
(Check when read)

(Check applicable portion when read)
_____ a.) if you are under the influence of alcohol,
_____ b.) if you are under the influence of hazardous or controlled substances

or to determine the presence of a controlled substance or it's metabolite listed in schedule I or II, other than marijuana or tetrahydrocannabinols.

_____ 2.   Refusal to take a test is a crime.
(Check when read)

_____ 3.   **(READ <u>ONLY</u> IF PROBABLE CAUSE TO BELIEVE VIOLATION OF CRIMINAL**
(Check **IF** read)   **VEHICULAR HOMICIDE AND INJURY LAWS) Because** I also have probable cause to believe you have violated the criminal vehicular

homicide or injury laws, a test will be taken with or without your consent.

_____ 4.   Before making your decision about testing, you have the right to consult with an

(Check when read)   attorney. If you wish to do so, a telephone and directory will be made available to you.
If you are unable to contact an attorney, you must make the decision on your own. You must make your decision within a reasonable period of time.

_____ 5.   If the test is unreasonably delayed or if you refuse to make a decision, you will be

(Check when read)   considered to have refused the test.

Do you understand what I have just explained? _____

Do you wish to consult with an attorney? _____

Time telephone made available: Start: _____
Stopped: _____

Will you take the (Breath) (Blood or Urine) test? _____

(If person refuses:)
What is your reason for refusing?_____

Name of Officer: _____
Time Completed: _____
                    (PRINT name of officer)
Date: _____

Courtesy of Major Michael L. Asleson, Minnesota State Patrol

Appendix D

IMPLIED CONSENT LAW
PEACE OFFICER'S CERTIFICATE

(PLEASE TYPE OR PRINT LEGIBLY, CROSS OUT REFERENCES TO INAPPLICABLE ITEMS.)

I certify to the Commissioners of Public Safety, State of Minnesota, that:

1. **I am a "peace officer" within the meaning of Minnesota Statutes Section 169A.03, Subdivision 18.**

2. **On (Date) _____ , I had probable cause to believe that the person named below has been driving,**

   operating or physically controlling a motor vehicle in violation of Minnesota Statutes Section 169A.20 within the State of Minnesota on _____ in _____ County.

Full Name		Date of Birth
Address		City, State, Zip
Driver License Number	License Plate or Registration Number	State of Issue

3. Reason for initial contact:
   - ☐ Vehicle stopped by officer because:
   - ☐ Accident   ☐ Vehicle already stopped (describe):
   - ☐ Other (describe):

4. Probable cause that person was driving, operating or in physical control:
   - ☐ Saw person   ☐ Person admitted   ☐ Other:

5. Probable cause that person was under influence (In addition to other information):
   - ☐ Odor of alcohol ☐ Bloodshot, watery eyes ☐ Slurred speech
   - ☐ Poor balance ☐ Admission
   - ☐ Other (describe)

6. Check at least one of the following:

   ☐ DWI arrest   ☐ Accident   ☐ Refused PBT   ☐

Failed PBT with AC of .08 or more

7. Other pertinent information

8. This person was requested to submit to a test to the provisions of the Minnesota Statutes Sections 169A.50-.53, and was read the attached Implied Consent Advisory on the other side of this form by: (Name and Agency)

9. The person: (X APPLICABLE BOX)

   ☐ Refused to provide a test sample to determine the presence of alcohol or hazardous or controlled substance or it's metabolite.

   ☐ Provided a sample blood, breath or urine which indicated an alcohol concentration of .08 or more.

   ☐ Provided a sample blood or urine which indicated the presence of a hazardous substance or schedule I or II controlled substance or it's metabolite, other than marijuana or THC.

Attach Notice of Revocation (Form PS31123) if issued, test results, and police reports.	Signature of Peace Officer
	Printed Name of Peace Officer
	Badge Number
	Business Telephone Number Date

MEDICAL PERSONNEL CERTIFICATE

Pursuant to Minn. Statutes Section 634.15, I certify as follows:
At the request of the undersigned officer, I withdrew a sample of
blood from:

NAME: _____

AT: _____
(location)

I am authorized and qualified to draw blood samples pursuant to
Minn. Statutes Section 169A.51, Subdivision 7.

I withdrew the sample of blood at _____ A.M./P.M.
after preparing the site of withdrawal with a non-alcohol
substance.

I used a sterile needle and container in withdrawing and receiving
the blood sample.

I gave the blood sample to the undersigned peace officer:

DATE: _____   _____
Signature

_____
Printed name

OCCUPATION (check applicable)
_____ Physician
_____ Registered Nurse
_____ Medical Technician
_____ Medical Technologist
_____ Laboratory Assistant
_____ Medical Laboratory Technician
_____ EMT/Paramedic

_____
Signature of Peace Officer

SEND WITH COPY OF ALCOHOL INFLUENCE REPORT, ARREST
OR ACCIDENT REPORT, INTOXILIZER RECORDS,
LABORATORY REPORT TO:

Department of Public Safety
Driver and Vehicle Services Division
Implied Consent Section
445 Minnesota Street, Suite 170
St. Paul, MN 55101-5170

The sample was submitted for analysis to:

Name of Agency, Analyst or Breath Test Operator
Address of Agency or Analyst
City, State, Zip
Sample Identification Number (Blood or Urine Tests Only)

PS1802-16

Courtesy of Major Michael L. Asleson, Minnesota State Patrol

ASPATORE